What others are saying about this book:

"What a timely book—just what is needed to successfully apply for a federal job or write an effective resume. This is a valuable resource for first-time job seekers and federal employees seeking promotions, lateral transfers, or detail assignments. I highly recommend it!"

—Frank T. Davis, President, Frank T. Davis Associates, and former Special Assistant to the Comptroller General of the United States

"Applying for Federal Jobs saves the day for both the novice and experienced federal job hunter who face today's "reinvented" federal job application. It really delivers with practical advice and how-to's for job-winning applications. Newcomers will appreciate the special federal hiring terms glossary. Managers and those with management aspirations can all profit from the advice for reaching the senior executive service."

—Judelle A. McArdle, President, of Federal Research Services.

"Pat Wood really knows her stuff. If you're a 'Fed' (or wannabe), you'll do well to buy her book and pay attention to what she has to say, especially about filling out the application forms and supplemental statements."

—Donna J. Moore, Career consultant and author of *Take Charge of Your Own Career, A Guide to Federal Employment*

What others said about Ms. Wood's other books:

"One of the 'Best of the Best' education and career print book materials."

—National Education and Information Center Advisory Committee

Other books by Patricia B. Wood

The 171 Reference Book
New Edition
Copyright 1991

The 171 Reference Book
Revised Edition
Copyright 1986

The 171 Workbook
Copyright 1978, 1979, 1981

The 171 Writing Portfolio (1991 edition)
Copyright 1991

Promote Yourself! How to Use Your Knowledge, Skills, and Abilities...and
Advance in the Federal Government
Copyright 1988

Order *The 171 Reference Book, The 171 Writing Portfolio* and *Promote*
Yourself! from:
Workbooks, Inc.
9039 Sligo Creek Parkway, #316
Silver Spring, MD 20901
Phone/FAX (301) 565-9467

APPLYING FOR FEDERAL JOBS

A Guide to Writing Successful Applications and Resumes
for the Job You Want in Government

Patricia B. Wood

BOOKHAVEN PRESS
Moon Township, PA

APPLYING FOR FEDERAL JOBS

A Guide to Writing Successful Applications and Resumes
For the Job You Want in Government

By Patricia B. Wood

Copyright © **1995 by Patricia B. Wood**

Printed and bound in the United States of America on acid free paper

Published by
BOOKHAVEN PRESS
401 Amherst Avenue
Moon Township, PA 15108

Disclaimer of All Warranties and Liabilities

The author and publisher make no warranties, either expressed or implied, with respect to the information contained herein. The information about periodicals and job services reported in this book is based on facts conveyed by their publishers and operators either in writing or by telephone interview. The author and publisher shall not be liable for any incidental or consequential damages in connection with, or arising out of, the use of material in this book.

Library of Congress Cataloging-in-Publication Data

Wood, Patricia B.
    Applying for federal jobs : a guide to writing successful applications and resumes for the job you want in government / by Patricia B. Wood.
        p.   cm.
    Includes bibliographical references and index.
    ISBN 0-943641-11-X (pbk. : alk. Paper)
    1. Civil service positions—United States. 2. Resumes
(Employment)—United States.   I. Title.
JK716.W66   1995
650.14—dc20   95-7816
                                                          CIP

For information on distribution or quantity discount rates, Telephone 412/262-5578 or write to: Sales Department, Bookhaven Press, P.O. Box 1243, Moon Township, PA 15108. Distributed to the trade by LOGIN Publishers Consortium, 1436 W. Randolph, Chicago, IL 60607, Tel. 1-800-626-4330. Library distributors include Quality Books, Unique Books, and Baker & Taylor.

Table of Contents

Introduction

Who Should Use This Book?

This book is for you if you are a U.S. citizen interested in applying for a job at any salary level with the federal government. That means:

- College students or graduates of any age,
- People who didn't go to college but have work or volunteer experience that would qualify them for federal employment,
- Current federal employees who want promotions, and
- Former federal employees who want to be rehired.

This book is also for those in business or government who help people find jobs or information about jobs. That means college placement counselors, career guidance counselors, career consultants, personnel officials, librarians, and anyone else who guides, coaches, counsels, or dispenses information about careers.

Like the civil service system, this book is an equal opportunity publication. Its tips will apply to you whatever your politics, race, color, religion, national origin, sex, marital status, or handicapping condition.

What Is This Book About?

Mainly, this book is about writing application forms and resumes to target and get the job you want in the federal government. It's about making sure your application stands out from the paper mountain that appears when a federal job is announced. This book offers step-by-step guidance, real-life and composite examples, and a federal career vocabulary (buzz words) to use in completing the government's new Optional Form 612 or in writing a federal-style resume that conforms to the government's hiring requirements. This book is also about developing a job search strategy so that you don't just fill out application forms and wait. You want to climb to the top of the paper mountain; you want an application that shouts from the mountain top: "Hire ME. I'm the best person for this job!"

I can promise you a hard climb. Competition is tough. Look to this book for some of the tips that can give you a competitive edge. The rest is up to you.

A Word About the Federal Hiring Climate

 The Clinton Administration, with much bipartisan support in Congress, is busy reinventing government, based on the Vice President's National Performance Review recommendations in 1993. The government reinvention effort is boldly trying to cut red tape, use new technologies, and serve its customers better.

Of course, the Clinton Administration and the new 104th Congress also intend to make government leaner, in programs and people. And what does becoming leaner mean to the job seeker? It means the same thing it does in corporate America, which is laying people off, downsizing, and restructuring like mad. The industrial age is gone. Both industry and government are well into the global information age. Even the experts aren't sure exactly what will shake out in terms of our social and economic structures and how we'll do our work in the future. While all this is happening, we can't go back to bed and pull the covers over our heads. We have to keep working and that means looking for jobs. The federal government is a big organization with almost 3 million employees. Even if the feds drop a few hundred thousand people as it turns some programs over to states, sells some activities to the private sector, or just lets some programs go, there will be some hiring in the federal sector. Even as this is written, for example, the FBI has announced plans to hire hundreds of new agents. Plus, there will be new hiring in state government and business as they pick up what the federal government relinquishes. Today astute job hunters have to be aware of what's going on in all sectors.

The New Federal Hiring Process and Tools

Luckily, as part of the reinvention effort, the federal government is trying to make it easier for the federal job seeker. Not easier to get a job, but easier to get yourself certified as "qualified" and easier to get information about where the jobs are.

This book explains the new federal hiring process and tools, including:

- Decentralized recruiting and hiring.
- Job hunter choices in written applications starting in 1995—the new optional form, a resume, or even the traditional Standard Form 171,

which is no longer a requirement for federal employment or promotion.
- Telephone and optical scan applications for a few jobs now and a growing number of jobs in the future.
- Instantaneous, 24-hour a day, online information about world-wide federal job vacancies, updated daily.

These are welcome, long overdue improvements in federal hiring. I

commend the employment "re-engineers" at the Office of Personnel Management for overseeing the transformation and for mobilizing the federal personnel community to enact these momentous changes.

A Federal Resume by Any Other Name Is a Form

What the federal government means by "resume" is not what is meant in the private sector. A federal-style resume is a federal form without a format. Here's what happened. First, the old one-size-fits-all Standard Form 171 was pared down, emerging as the new Optional Form 612, to be customized to fit an announced job. Job hunters may now use either form. If you choose not to use one of these forms, you may use a resume, but you must include all the information that appears on the new form, including your social security number and other details that you would never put on a short, industrial-strength resume. Voila—a federal-style resume.

Since the federal government had no experience with resumes until 1995, it is not a part of the exciting electronic job search and resume revolution described by career columnist Joyce Lain Kennedy and business editor Thomas J. Morrow in their 1994 co-written books on this subject. In this new world, resume-writing rules have changed. Computers scan thousands of resumes for keywords (nouns, not verbs), neatly file applications by job possibilities in multiple electronic in-boxes, and whip out an appropriate few when a private sector manager has an opening.

That's not to say the federal government doesn't have an electronic recruiting/screening revolution underway. It does, but it's based on precisely-designed questionnaires and optical scan *forms,* not resumes. Electronic scanners can screen and rate up to 25 applications per minute. These private sector and federal applicant screening technologies are driven by the same force: the waste of using hordes of human beings to read hundreds, or even thousands, of paper resumes and applications for announced jobs. Computers are faster and more objective. Private sector employers may be able to lose, forget, hide or neglect a resume, but Uncle Sam has a legal obligation to give each applicant the same opportunity to be screened and hired under the competitive civil service. These electronic technologies will become more and more important in the future federal hiring process. For now, we are in a major transition period.

Is There a Test for Federal Hiring?

The federal government is reducing its dependence on "written" tests, but there is a test for federal hiring. It's the federal application form or resume—the test that you write yourself. This book, *Applying for Federal Jobs, A Guide to Writing Successful Applications and Resumes for the Job You Want in Government*, will help you pass the test.

Patricia B. Wood
Silver Spring, MD
January 1995

Chapter One
A New Day, A New Way

Y ears ago, 1978 to be exact, I wrote my first book on the federal hiring system and how to fill out the application for federal employment. The first of its kind, *The 171 Workbook* was renamed *The 171 Reference Book* as I updated it through the years. The book got its name from the number of the official federal application form, Standard Form 171. Printed in green ink, this four-page form became one of the most familiar — and despised — forms used by government employees. It was the form that got you in, and it was also the form that got you promoted.

Federal Hiring Procedures Have Changed

In the years since my first book, many things about the hiring process have changed, including abolishing the old form as a requirement for federal employment. Starting in 1995, job hunters may use resumes, a new Optional Form 612, or whatever they wish to apply for a job, including the abolished form! It's up to the applicant. Many more changes are underway based on the Vice President's National Performance Review recommendations in 1993 to rid government of its endless red tape, flatten the enormous top-heavy hierarchies, and improve services to the American people at less cost. Many of these proposed reforms are already underway with considerable bipartisan support in the Congress. Reforms include fully decentralizing the hiring process and making job information more accessible and hiring procedures less cumbersome for those who are interested in a federal career. It's about time!

S tarting in 1995, job hunters may use resumes.

Civil Service Hasn't Changed

With so many changes underway, it's also time for a new book about the federal hiring process and the new ways to present your qualifications for a federal job. The first thing to understand is that the fundamental underpinnings of federal employment in the executive branch of government have not changed. The civil service system, a competitive hiring system used for new hires and promotions, is alive and well. In this system, people are hired on merit as measured against established standards or specific job requirements. The competitive service is based on principles of fair and equitable treatment without regard to your politics, race, color, religion, national origin, sex, marital status, age, or handicapping conditions.

Who Am I to Be Writing a Book Like This?

Let me give you my credentials for writing books about federal hiring procedures. To begin with, I'm not an expert on the federal personnel system and I don't ever expect to be. The system, even a reinvented, simplified one, is still complex.

When I wrote my first book, I wasn't in the government. I planned to move from Atlanta to Washington, DC, and I wanted a federal public affairs job. In those days — the late 70s — the hiring system was very centralized. First you had to fill out an application form (one form for mid-level positions and the Standard Form 171 for senior level positions) and send it to the Civil Service Commission (now the Office of Personnel Management). The Civil Service Commission examined your credentials and gave you a rating. Your name went on a centralized register (list of qualified people) for a certain kind of job. Most people stopped at that and just waited. They waited a long time. It wasn't a great system. Actually, your rating was a kind of "license" to go job hunting, but most federal job hunters didn't seem to know that.

A Job Offer Resulted from My First Try

In my case, I filled out both forms but didn't wait to get my "hunting license." I dropped the applications in the mailbox and made a quick trip to Washington to start looking around. I began by making calls to agencies from my hotel room starting with the "A's" in the phone book. It didn't take long before I got a nibble — a job vacancy in the Department of Agriculture. A friendly personnel specialist told me that yes, there was an opening for a public information specialist. I asked for, and she gave me, the name of the person doing the hiring. It was near the end of the work day when I called. His secretary had already gone home, and he answered the phone. I asked about the job, throwing in the fact that I had, as a teenager, been State President of the 4-H Club. (The 4-H Clubs are overseen by the Extension Service, a part of the Department of Agriculture.)

He asked me to come to his office the next day for an interview. I had a good feeling about our meeting. He obviously liked me and my writing samples. At his request I left a copy of the applications I had mailed to the

Civil Service Commission. Within a few weeks he called me in Atlanta and offered me the job. I learned a lot from that experience — mainly, if you can find the job, the person doing the hiring will help you get through the system. Unfortunately, although I had acted in good faith, I didn't take the job. I wasn't quite ready to relocate because everything happened so fast.

My Daughter Got a Job Offer and I Got Inspired

I moved to Washington, DC, the next year, followed by my daughter when she graduated from college. She had written a resume and an SF-171 with a little help from me and was pounding the pavement in D.C. to sell herself in person. Like me, mainly by making herself visible, she also got a federal job offer (which she also declined because she got an offer she liked better in medical research).

While my daughter was on her job hunting rounds, a federal personnel specialist told her she had an excellent application (an application good enough to get her a grade level rating from the Civil Service Commission that was two grades higher than the usual college graduate). He mentioned in passing that he wished he had time to write a book about the SF-171. When my daughter told me, I thought, "I have time. I'll write the book." And I did. I had three main points to make, points that I have made a consistent theme in books over the years.

❶   Learn enough about the hiring system to make it work for you.

❷   Write an application in plain English that emphasizes your skills and accomplishments for a particular job or line of work.

❸   Sell yourself in person as well as on paper.

The first book was a big hit and, by the way, got me another federal job offer. I had sent copies to several people I knew in government. A few months later one of these officials called me to ask if I would like a temporary job in the public affairs office writing that agency's annual report. I was interested and sent in the necessary SF-171 to be processed by the agency. Remember, then as now, my name had to appear on a list of qualified applicants before I could be hired.

After only a few months in that temporary job, I got a surprise call. Apparently my name was still on a central register at the Civil Service Commission, based on the applications I had mailed from Atlanta a couple of years before. If interested, I was asked to come in to interview for a job as a speech writer in the Department of Health and Human Services. I got the job offer, and at that point I had a choice. I could take this potentially permanent job at the same grade (salary) level as the temporary job or, since my temporary employer wanted me around longer, I could move into another temporary job in that agency at a higher level. I chose the permanent job, and it led to a fulfilling career in the federal government. My career has included much exposure to the application process as I have revised my own SF-171 for promotions or challenging lateral transfers. And as a manager, I have been responsible for hiring and promoting dozens of employees. I have also coached staff and colleagues on how to write applications and resumes to achieve their career aspirations. I've built a lot of my personal knowledge and experience into this book.

Shorter, Friendlier, Easier Federal Hiring System

The federal hiring process has been slowly changing since I became a federal employee in 1978. A March 1994 report of the Merit Systems Protection Board says that the hiring process has steadily been decentralized over the past 10 or 15 years to the point that federal agencies already control the process used to staff 80 percent of professional and administrative positions. But changes are moving much faster now that the Office of Personnel Management (the successor to the Civil Service Commission) is moving to implement the systemic changes recommended as a result of the National Performance Review initiative to reinvent government.

The Office of Personnel Management, in collaboration with personnel officials from all over government, is decentralizing the rest of the federal hiring process to federal agencies and trying to make it shorter, easier and friendlier for the job seeker. Decentralization means that the Office of Personnel Management will delegate to federal departments and independent agencies complete authority to hire new people and promote their own employees, based on merit systems that these organizations will set up. Some of these changes will require Congressional action and will take time, but the Office of Personnel Management is busy drafting legislation right now. Its role will be to oversee the merit systems that the agencies will set up, offer expanded personnel support systems to the agencies, and provide a comprehensive, user-friendly, state-of-the-art electronic job information network for job seekers. We're moving into the 21st Century—it's a new day, a new way!

Government Is Downsizing, Times Are Tough, So What About You?

Since you are reading this book, chances are you on the outside of government and are considering federal employment, or you are a federal employee caught in the middle of a changing work environment. Your agency may be downsizing (reducing its staff), offering buyouts, restructuring its business operations, and flattening the organization (cutting the number of supervisors and managers). It's tough. You were hoping for a promotion, and now you're wondering if your job is going to be changed or abolished. I'm writing for both of you, the outsider who doesn't know anything about the system at all and the insider who's watching — and maybe confused about — an old system that's being re-invented. If you aren't a federal employee, I hope you will bear with me while I explain some of the changes to the application process. You don't care what *was*, you want to know what *is*. The problem, however, is that much of the process is in transition. Some things are in the process of *becoming* so we have to keep the connection with the way things *were* so we'll understand what *will be*.

Make sure your application says "Hire me, I'm the best person for this job."

I'll try not to overwhelm you — mainly because you don't need to know everything, you just need to know the basics of the system and some key points about how to present your qualifications for specific jobs so that you'll be invited for an interview. Almost every federal job opening attracts applications from many highly qualified people. You want to make sure your application says "Hire me, I'm the best person for this job!"

This Book Will Help You Edge Out the Competition

I'm writing this book to help you describe your skills and experience in the most eye-catching, readable way possible to edge out the competition so that you can get the job you want. And I will try to make another point very clear: Despite the many changes underway in the hiring process, one thing has not changed: You must visibly and actively pursue jobs, not just send in an application and wait.

I hope this book will be as helpful and as popular as my first book and its subsequent revisions. One of my readers wrote me recently: "Are you going to publish a new book? I want to be the first in line to get it." Yes, here's the new book. Use it! And I hope you're first in line for the job you want.

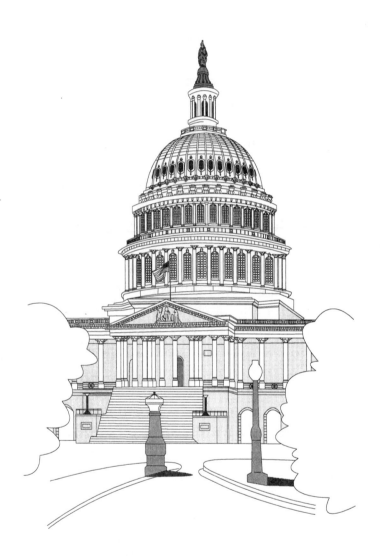

Chapter Two
Working For The
Nation's Largest Employer

The federal government is the nation's largest employer. It has more employees than the first 16 of the Fortune 500 companies added together. Its 2.9 million civilian employees do every kind of job imaginable.

What Federal Workers Do and Where They Work

Federal employees have walked on the moon, launched space explorations, and discovered the AIDS virus. Every day, federal workers provide health care to our veterans, guard our borders, control pollution in the environment, look after our national parks, deliver mail, and dispense old age and survivors' benefits to millions of Americans.

Among the ranks of federal employees you'll find statisticians, actuaries, accountants, engineers, radiologists, pharmacists, lawyers, law enforcement officers, secretaries, computer technicians, librarians, social workers, management analysts, economists, artists, warehouse workers, researchers, bus drivers, geologists, teachers, and morticians. In all, there are more than 1,000 occupations. Federal employees work in offices, warehouses, shipyards, national parks, hospitals, laboratories, embassies, military bases, and many other places all over the country and in many foreign posts.

With the recent advent of telecommuting, a few federal employees now work from home or a telework center for part of their work week. Certain jobs that are computer and phone intensive—like budget analyst or writer/editor—are the kinds of jobs that can be done at home for at least part of the time. The Department of Transportation, with its interest in keeping cars off the highways, is taking a leadership role in developing alternatives to traditional commuting.

A few federal employees now work from home or a telework center.

More than two-thirds of all full-time federal civilian employees work in four large Executive Branch departments: Defense, Veterans Affairs, Treasury (which houses the Internal Revenue Service), and Health and Human Services (which housed the Social Security Administration until

March 1995 when it became an independent agency). These figures don't include the 700,000 employees of the Postal Service, which has a separate hiring system.

The vast majority of federal employees work in large metropolitan areas in this country. About 390,000 federal civilian employees work in the Washington, DC Metropolitan Area. Among states, California has the largest number of civilian, non-postal employees—about 190,000. Metropolitan areas with more than 40,000 employees are the Philadelphia-New York corridor, the Norfolk-Virginia Beach-Portsmouth area, and Baltimore. Areas with more than 25,000 employees are Atlanta, Chicago, Los Angeles-Long Beach, San Antonio, New York City, San Diego, and Denver.

But federal workers are also found in small towns and hamlets. Just look in the blue pages of your phone directory. In fact, as a percentage of their total working population, many small towns beat out Washington, DC. About 12 percent of the workers in DC are federal employees; but that's not as big as the percentage of federal workers in Liberty County, GA or Daggett County, Utah, according to Mike Causey, a *Washington Post* reporter who writes a column called *The Federal Diary*.

Most federal organizations are undergoing serious downsizing efforts. This is a response to public demand for less government and the current effort by the Clinton Administration and the Congress to not only reinvent the way our government does business, but also change some of the things that government does. In 1993 the Administration pledged to reduce the federal workforce by about 252,000 civilian employees by 1999, but the President and the Congress later increased that figure to almost 273,000. The major target was not front line workers, but what the National Performance Review called "positions of over control and micromanagement." The new Republican-dominated Congress of 1995 will seek even deeper reductions.

The same thing is going on in the private sector. To survive, many corporations are reducing the size of their workforce. The fact that the government is downsizing should not discourage you from applying for federal jobs. Flexible people, who continue to learn and grow and whose job hunting skills are honed to perfection, will get the available jobs or promotions in both sectors. Even with federal staff reductions already underway in 1994, the executive branch hired 366,418 people, according to workforce statistics from the Office of Personnel Management. Of this number, 290,590 were new hires (people who are not current civilian employees).

How Jobs Are Classified and Paid

If you want a job in the federal government, you need to understand the basics of how jobs are classified and paid. That way you will know what kind of job to aim for and what salary to expect. In the government, your salary depends on what kind of job you are in, not what your overall qualifications may be.

Like the rest of the federal personnel system, the Job Classification and Pay System is currently undergoing scrutiny by top level government and federal union officials. The Vice President's National Performance Review recommended overhauling the whole classification system.

The Vice President's National Performance Review recommended overhauling the whole classification system.

People Are Boxed In

The current complex classification system has 459 job series (kinds of work), 15 grades (levels of difficulty), and 10 steps in each grade. This adds up to thousands of classified jobs—each in its own little box with a specific salary. When this system was set up, a federal worker was supposed to do the specific work defined in his or her box at a set grade level.

Thus in each federal job you knew exactly what box you were in and what you were supposed to do. You could get promoted to a position with more responsibility and go to the next box up, you could get transferred to a lateral box and move to another position at the same level of difficulty, or you could go down. There are lots of reasons for going down a box or two—changing career fields and having to start at a lower level, being bumped down because of a reduction-in-force (someone with more seniority gets your job and bumps you down), or for personal reasons, such as getting married and moving to another location with no open positions in your field at your grade level.

This system is so precise and so complex that it takes more than 50,000 personnel specialists and thousands of pages of laws, regulations, and personnel guidelines to administer. With the advent of the reinventing government recommendations from the National Performance Review, most of the 10,000-page personnel guide has been abolished, and personnel specialists are a primary target of first-round staff reductions. This complicated personnel system may have worked well at a time when our country's government mimicked industry's assembly lines. But assembly lines don't fit anymore in a dynamic, rapidly changing world, including the federal work environment. It's hard—and pointless—to keep federal workers in boxes. A lower level employee with a computer and a modem often has access to more information than a supervisor who hasn't come to grips with the electronic age. Today in government, the trend is toward generalists rather than narrowly-focused specialists. In addition, the trend toward teams, with shared responsibilities and sometimes rotating leadership, is breaking down the invisible walls of a rigid classification system.

Government Is Experimenting with Change

Government reformers in management and federal unions are already developing legislative proposals to implement personnel recommendations made by the National Performance Review. These reforms would include giving agencies flexibility in classifying jobs and paying employees. Several federal agencies have been experimenting with simpler systems over a number of years. In the China Lake Experiment in California, the Navy took its civilian employees out of their boxes. They classified all jobs in just five career paths—professional, technical, specialist, administrative and clerical—and then folded all General Schedule grades into four, five, or six pay bands within each career path. This demonstration also allowed federal managers to pay market salaries to recruit people and to increase the pay of outstanding employees without having to promote them.

The above discussion is about recommendations, experiments and trends related to job classification and pay. For now, and probably for some time into the future, the longtime Federal Classification and Pay System still exists, so let's take a look.

The federal classification system looks at a job in two ways—the kind of work (series) and the level of difficulty (grade). Federal pay is directly tied to the classification system. Most professional, administrative, technical, and clerical positions are paid under a General Schedule based on job classification. The Fiscal Year 1995 pay schedule is shown on the next page.

The General Schedule applies to about 75 percent of all federal civilian non-postal employees. Under the schedule, positions are graded from GS-1 to GS-15. A GS-12 public information specialist in St. Louis is considered to be at the same level of difficulty as a GS-12 customs inspector in Miami although the kind of work they do (the series) may be very different.

The Federal Employees Pay Comparability Act of 1990 is phasing in changes in the pay system, including locality pay (special raises of up to 8 percent for workers in high-cost cities like Los Angeles or New York).

TABLE 2-1
ANNUAL SALARY RATES
1995 General Schedule (GS)

STEP INCREASES 1-10										
GRADE	1	2	3	4	5	6	7	8	9	10
GS-1	12,595	13,015	13,433	13,851	14,272	14,517	14,929	15,343	15,365	15,754
2	14,161	14,498	14,968	15,365	15,534	15,990	16,447	16,903	17,360	17,816
3	15,452	15,968	16,583	16,999	17,514	18,030	18,546	19,061	19,577	20,092
4	17,346	17,924	18,502	19,080	19,658	20,236	20,813	21,391	21,969	22,547
5	19,407	20,054	20,701	21,349	21,996	22,643	23,291	23,938	24,585	25,233
6	21,632	22,353	23,074	23,795	24,516	25,237	25,958	26,679	27,400	28,121
7	24,038	24,838	25,639	26,440	27,241	28,042	28,843	29,644	30,445	31,245
8	26,662	27,509	28,396	29,283	30,170	31,057	31,944	32,837	33,718	38,605
9	29,405	30,385	31,366	32,346	33,326	34,307	35,287	36,268	37,248	38,228
10	32,382	33,462	34,542	35,622	36,702	37,782	38,862	39,942	41,022	42,102
11	35,578	36,763	37,949	39,135	40,321	41,506	42,692	43,878	45,064	46,249
12	42,641	44,063	45,484	46,905	48,326	49,747	51,169	52,590	54,001	55,432
13	50,706	52,396	54,086	55,776	57,466	59,156	60,846	62,536	64,225	65,915
14	59,920	61,917	63,914	65,911	67,908	69,905	71,902	73,899	75,896	77,893
15	70,482	72,832	75,181	77,531	79,881	82,231	84,580	86,930	89,280	91,629

Wage Grade System

Federal blue collar workers, the majority of whom work as civilians for the Armed Forces, already receive pay based on local hourly rates under the Wage Grade (WG) pay system. Grades range from WG-1 to WG-19. This book is not focused on jobs in the Wage Grade System, although the themes of writing plain English applications and selling yourself in person apply. You may wish to consult *Guide to Federal Technical, Trades and Labor Jobs*, published by Resource Directories, Suite 301, 3361 Executive Parkway, Toledo, OH 43606, (800) 274-8515. This 1992 guide may be the only reference book that specializes in blue collar and non-professional federal jobs that do not require a college degree.

Senior Executive Service

The Senior Executive Service (SES) is a separate personnel and pay system for about 7,800 men and women who set policy and administer programs at the highest level of the Executive Branch. SES covers most executive, managerial and other policy-making jobs. Their responsibilities are greater than positions in the General Schedule, and this difference is reflected in bigger paychecks. See Chapter 10 for more information about the SES.

Excepted Agencies

Some federal agencies are excepted from the competitive civil service. The largest of these is the U.S. Postal Service, with its 700,000 employees. Others are the Federal Bureau of Investigation and the Central Intelligence Agency. You'll find a list of excepted agencies in the Appendices. These organizations have their own hiring systems, but all are based on a competitive merit system.

Position Classification Standards

Now that we've looked at job classification by pay, let's look at how jobs are sorted by the kinds of work to be done. The Office of Personnel Management has sorted jobs into 22 different occupational groups, such as Accounting and Budget as one group and Engineering and Architecture as another. The list in Table 2-2 shows the 22 Occupational Groups.

You'll find the groups further sorted, with an explanation of what is done in each series (kind of position) at each grade (level of difficulty) in a lengthy set of volumes called *Position Classification Standards*. You'll find these standards in most federal personnel offices and in Federal Employment Information Centers over the country.

The occupational groups and the job series are numerical. The closer the numbers are to each other, the more alike the positions are. For example, in the Biological Sciences Group (GS-0400), horticulturist and forester are more closely related to each other than they are related to the Accounting and Budgeting Group (GS-0500), where you will find accountant and tax examiner. Most job opportunities are in the General Administration, Clerical, and Office Services Group (GS-0300).

TABLE 2-2
OCCUPATIONAL GROUPS

GS-000: Miscellaneous
GS-100: Social Science, Psychology, and Welfare
GS-200: Personnel Management and Industrial Relations Group
GS-300: General Administrative, Clerical, and Office Services Group
GS-400: Biological Science
GS-500: Accounting and Budget
GS-600: Medical, Hospital, Dental, and Public Health
GS-700: Veterinary Medical Science Group
GS-800: Engineering and Architecture
GS-900: Legal and Kindred Group
GS-1000: Information and Arts
GS-1100: Business and Industry
GS-1200: Copyright, Patent, and Trade-Mark
GS-1300: Physical Science
GS-1400: Library and Archives
GS-1500: Mathematics and Statistics
GS-1600: Equipment, Facilities, and Services Group
GS-1700: Education
GS-1800: Investigation
GS-1900: Quality Assurance, Inspection, and Grading
GS-2000: Supply
GS-2100: Transportation

Table 2-3 shows the 20 occupations for which the largest number of college graduates were hired in Fiscal Year 1992. The source is *Working for US in the 1990's*, U.S. Department of Labor, Bureau of Labor Statistics (taken from the Summer 1993 issue of *Occupational Quarterly*).

TABLE 2-3
NEW HIRES BY OCCUPATION IN FISCAL YEAR 1992

Occupations	GS Series Number	New Hires FY 92
Computer Specialists	334	1,140
General Attorneys	905	917
Nurses	610	901
Miscellaneous Administrators and Analysts	301	805
Financial Institution Examiners	570	797
Medical Officers	602	674
Auditors	511	603
Electronics Engineers	855	566
Civil Engineers	810	558
Criminal Investigators	1811	538
General Engineers	801	486
Accountants	510	443
General Educators and Trainers	1701	438
Management / Program Analysts	343	382
Contracting Specialists	1102	369
Social Scientists	101	344
Medical Technologists	644	291
Social Workers	644	290
General Biological Scientists	401	290
Chemists	1320	282

In the age of reinvention, more and more government work requires people who can break out of their classification boxes, learn new things, and tackle a variety of tasks. Many government offices, as they are revising their missions and reengineering their work to be less bureaucratic and more customer-focused, are expecting workers to be more flexible, just as the jobs are becoming more flexible. These things are already happening in some agencies, even though it may take years for the classification system to catch up.

Qualification Standards

How do you find out how much experience and education are required for the job you want? These requirements are on the job announcement published by a federal organization when it has a vacancy. The announcement summarizes the minimum educational and work requirements and lists the selective factors (specific qualifications essential to the announced job). The agency examines the applicant's qualifications against these announced requirements. If you want to do more general research, you may consult the *Qualification Standards Handbook for General Schedule Positions*. It contains the minimum experience and educational standards for almost every federal job under that schedule. It's available in every federal personnel office, but other organizations have it also because the Government Printing Office sells it.

How An Agency Gives You Credit for Your Experience and Education

The Office of Personnel Management issued generic qualifications standards that are rather flexible. However, in general, you may qualify for an entry-level professional position (GS-5) with:

• a college degree, or

• 3 years of general experience (any work that offers a general background of work skills suitable for the broad area of work in the announced job), or

• a combination of education and experience equivalent to the above.

In the above example, a college graduate with superior academic achievement may qualify for a GS-7. Achievement is defined as the upper third of your class, a grade point average of 3.0 or better on a 4.0 scale, or membership in a national honor society.

As indicated above, education and experience may be combined to qualify you for a certain grade level. For example, you are applying for the position of Quality Assurance Specialist, GS-1910-5. You have 2 years of general experience and 45 semester hours in course work related to the job requirements. You meet 67 percent of the required experience and 38 percent of the required education. You exceed the total requirement and are considered "qualified" for the position.

The qualifications standards for a GS-9 position usually require:

- 2 full years of progressively higher graduate education, or

- a master's or equivalent degree, or

- 1 year of specialized experience (work that is very closely related to the announced job). This work must be the equivalent to at least a GS-7.

In theory, a feature of the federal merit system is that either experience or a combination of experience and education can qualify you for a position. What counts is where you are right now in terms of skills, not how you got there. In fact, a 1994 study revealed that being promoted in government seems to depend more on educational level than any other single factor. The Merit Systems Protection Board monitored the progress of 40,000 federal employees who came into government in 1984. Their report, *Entering Professional Positions in the Federal Government*, said that many of government's ablest workers came up through the ranks to professional and management jobs. Nevertheless, it found that college graduates were more likely to be promoted and to be promoted faster than those who did not graduate.

Changing Your Job Series

It's not uncommon for a person to qualify for several kinds of jobs. If you are a federal employee who wants to change the kind of work you do, consult the Position Classification Standards in your personnel office to learn what is done in positions in the new field of work, and what experience and education you must have to make the transition. Because of transferable skills, sometimes these transitions can be made very easily. Again, how you got these skills must be documented on your application.

If you are in a clerical position and wish to change to another job series, you cannot draw upon your clerical duties to make the transition.

However, other than clerical functions, even if you are in a clerical position, can be used. You may also use training, education, special assignments, volunteer work, and other experience to get the skills required for nonclerical positions. Legislation passed in 1994 removed a previous barrier to upward mobility for federal employees. Previously, a person in any federal job could not obtain training at federal expense for skills not needed in that position. This short-sighted policy may have made sense once, but it no longer fits a working environment that must respond quickly to public demands and expectations of government programs. Today it makes sense to train or retrain public employees to do work that is looming on the horizon. If you are a federal employee, your supervisor may not be aware of this change in policy, but your personnel office should have the guidelines on this proviso in the Federal Workforce Restructuring Act of 1994.

College graduates were more likely to be promoted.

Many agencies have developmental programs that help secretaries and other support staff move into professional positions. If you are a federal employee, go to your supervisor or a personnel counselor to help you identify and get the skills you need to change jobs, if that is your goal. Don't be discouraged. Many people have made this transition and you can too, if you demonstrate that you have the qualifying skills.

How Federal Agencies Hire

Each agency has its own way of handling the legal complexities, processes, and paperwork for hiring and promoting people competitively. Similar forms will have different names and numbers from agency to agency. The hiring jargon may vary also. Even so, some basic steps apply throughout government.

Let's look at the federal hiring process from a manager's point of view within a federal agency. Work needs shift. New technologies come in. Employees retire or change jobs. These things mean that jobs are vacated or new jobs must be created. Managers must decide whether to open the competition to outside candidates or promote from within, but this decision depends on many things. At a big picture level, the agency may be downsizing and new hires aren't allowed. Also, the agency may have a personnel ceiling imposed by the Office of Management and Budget based on the agency's mission and budget.

Depending on these bigger considerations, a manager may have several choices about filling the position. Here are the choices (simplified):

①   **Move someone in from the same kind of job at the same grade level or from a higher grade if the employee is willing to take a "down grade".** This is a lateral transfer and can be done without a job announcement.

②   **Open the position to candidates with status.** These are current federal employees or former employees who can be rehired.

Such an announcement can be limited to a narrow or broad range of people depending on a variety of circumstances. For example, the job could be opened only to qualified applicants within that office, or within that agency. If the competition is limited to the agency, it could be opened to candidates in the local area or to candidates from that agency nationwide.

On a job announcement, the range of people to whom a job is open is listed under *area of consideration* or *distribution*. Only those people will be considered for the vacancy.

If managers know qualified people within their own offices or sections who would be qualified for promotion, they may wish to limit the area of consideration. The list generated will include these people if they apply for the position. In fact, this is often desirable from the manager's point of view because it offers promotional opportunities to a pool of qualified people who are already nearby and whose work is well known. However, with downsizing and other factors, the manager may be forced to limit the area of competition even if he or she would prefer to seek candidates from a bigger pool.

③   **Announce the job opening to any qualified applicant in or out of the government.**

In this case, even though the job is opened to both status and non-status candidates, the area of consideration could be limited to a certain geographical area. Thus, it's important for you to read carefully every part of a job announcement, especially the area of consideration and the qualifying factors, so that you do not waste your time in applying for jobs that are not available to you.

Announcing the Position

Personnel specialists within the agency are responsible for posting (announcing) the job. One of the most helpful recent improvements in the federal hiring process is an electronic system developed by the Office of Personnel Management that lists worldwide federal job vacancies. Personnel specialists all over government update this list daily. This is an incredible step forward for the job hunter and the agency. Before this development, personnel offices in agencies within the same departments of government (Housing and Urban Development, Health and Human Services, Agriculture, Labor, etc.) were not aware of the staffing needs or job postings in their sister agencies even if they were located in the same building. If a position is hard to fill, the agency might run an ad in the newspaper or recruit more aggressively than simply posting the job on the federal electronic database. Several private firms also collect and publish abbreviated federal job listings. We'll discuss both the federal and private sector job hunting resources in Chapter 8.

Evaluating and Hiring

Here's what happens when a job closes. Remember, the details may differ from agency to agency.

Screen   When a job closes, a personnel specialist gives a cursory review of all application packages to make sure that applicants are at least minimally qualified. The applications of those that aren't are screened out.

No manager hires someone he or she hasn't met.

Panel   Next, either the personnel office or the hiring office names three people to form a rating panel to carefully review the applications. These people are at least the same grade level as the announced job and are usually in the same field of work. Each member of the panel reviews the information in the application and any supporting documents against the announced criteria for the job. Usually the hiring office will have determined in advance exactly what factors should be evaluated and what weight the panel should give to each factor. The panel compares all the applications with each other and may interview the applicants. The panel comes up with a preliminary best-qualified list. In some agencies, the applicants receive numerical scores, based on the weights and factors. In other agencies, applicants are grouped into categories such as "best qualified" and "qualified."

Review   The personnel specialist reviews the work of the panel and develops a final list of best qualified applicants. This process includes adding any points appropriate for veterans (unless the job is for internal promotions).

Select   The manager who decided to fill a vacancy or set up a new job in the first place is the person who makes the hiring decision. The hiring official (or selecting official) makes a selection from the best qualified list. He or she may or may not interview the candidates. If the manager selects someone without interviewing, it's because he or she knows the candidate or may have been a part of the panel that did the interviewing. No manager hires someone he or she hasn't met.

Sometimes a manager will use a list to hire or promote more than one person, depending upon the number of vacant positions or other circumstances. This could happen even if the announcement specified that only one job was open. In other words, when a best-qualified list is created, managers can use it to fill other vacant jobs in that series at that grade level, even if these jobs are not announced.

Federal managers are almost always in the driver's seat as far as hiring goes. They know what jobs are available or could be created in their departments, divisions, sections, branches, or offices; they or their staff write the job descriptions; and they make the hiring decisions. Thus, an important part of your job-hunting strategy is to get ahead of the job announcements. It's okay to interview federal managers about their mission and activities. See Chapter 8.

Chapter Three
The New Federal
Application Process:
Not-So-Standard Forms and Technology

Uncle Sam is reinventing the federal hiring process. He wants to make it easier for you as a job hunter to get information about federal employment opportunities and to apply for a job. He's also trying to make it easier for the government to process the millions of applications that come in response to thousands of job announcements each year. To do this, Uncle Sam is simplifying the application process, introducing new technologies to make things faster for both the applicant and the government, and decentralizing much of the operation out of the Office of Personnel Management and into the hands of the agencies that have the vacancies.

The Information the Government Needs to Hire You

In order to hire you, a federal agency must collect information on your education, work experience, and personal background. An agency uses this information to decide if you are both qualified and fit for a federal job. Thus, applying for a federal job means not only supplying information about your experience and education (qualifications for the job), but also answering personal questions about your citizenship and other matters like past legal violations (suitability for a federal job).

From 1968 until 1994, the federal government required applicants to supply all this information up front on Standard Form 171. Beginning in 1995, this form is no longer required, although the federal government still wants much of the same basic information from you. Some of the information requested has been eliminated or pared down and you won't have to answer the personal questions in most cases until you've been narrowed down to one of the qualified candidates for the job. The new procedures were developed by the Office of Personnel Management, consulting with an interagency task force representing 16 federal departments and independent agencies. The Office of Personnel Management also got suggestions from personnel directors of more than 50 federal agencies, the

The SF-171 application form is now optional.

National Partnership Council (high level government and union officials), organizations representing major constituencies, and the general public.

New Federal Application Process and Forms

For you, the job hunter, the new federal application process has three major features:

1. New Forms

Two new optional forms and an information flyer called *Applying for a Federal Job* replace the instructions and the questions on the abolished SF-171. Copies of the two new forms and the flyer are at the end of this chapter. The Office of Personnel Management plans to make the flyer available in Braille, large print, audio tape, and computer disk.

The two forms are the *Optional Application for Federal Employment (OF 612)* and *Declaration for Federal Employment (OF 306)*. Some of the old questions were eliminated, and the information requested was streamlined to target a specific job. Even so, you still have a lot of information to supply. Basically, the two optional forms separate the qualifications questions from the suitability or fitness questions that were on the old SF-171:

>*Optional Application for Federal Employment* (OF 612)—asks personal questions to satisfy legal requirements (like citizenship and veterans' preference) and questions about your experience, education, and skills. This form is the primary subject of this book. You will find step-by-step instructions in Chapter 4.

>*Declaration for Federal Employment* (OF 306)—asks personal questions about felonies, court martials, loan defaults, and other things. (If you answer yes to these questions, you are not necessarily considered unsuitable for a federal job, but these factors are considered.) You have an opportunity on the form to explain the circumstances in each situation. Do not fill out this form as part of your initial application. Because so many people apply for every federal job, it's certainly an improvement in the federal hiring process not to burden applicants with these questions up front. (This form is self-explanatory and I do not include instructions or comments in this

book except for this: Be scrupulously honest in answering every question.)

Actually, agencies *could* ask you to complete this form at any time during the process, but the plan is that only the final few applicants who have a good chance of receiving a job offer would complete this form. This form is not optional if an agency asks you to complete this form. You must fill it out if you want the job.

2. Choices in Written Applications

You have a choice in what you use to submit a written application. You may use the Optional Form 612 (see Chapter 4), a resume (see Chapter 6), or even the old SF-171 if you happen to have electronic or paper copies available (see my book, *The 171 Reference Book, Revised Edition*). Whatever you choose to submit, you must include all the information asked for on the flyer and in the job announcement for the job you have targeted. If you don't, you won't be considered. The job announcement is key to the process. The agency can ask for any job-related information needed to evaluate candidates for the position and ask for any information required by law.

The job announcement is key to the process.

If you submit the SF-171, you do not have to answer the questions on page 4 of the form. These sensitive suitability questions are now included on the new *Declaration for Federal Employment*. Cross through these questions on the SF-171. You might also type N/A (not applicable) for other personal questions on the SF-171. These include questions 3 - 5 which ask for your sex, date of birth, and birthplace. Answer these kinds of questions, however, if the job announcement asks for this information. I suggest that you answer the other questions on the SF-171 that are not on the new *Optional Form 612*, such as questions on availability for travel and how many hours you wish to work.

3. Alternate Applications Using Technology

For certain jobs, you may use the telephone or automated techniques to submit qualifying information.

Telephone Application System (TAPS). You may apply for Professional Nurse and Border Patrol Agent using a touch-tone telephone. Other positions will be added in the future. Responses to the phone system, which is operated by the Office of Personnel Management, are transcribed and computer-rated against the qualifications standards. Eligible candidates are placed on a referral list within a day. Agencies may use this list when they have these kinds of jobs to fill. If an agency picks your name, you will still have to fill out forms or whatever the agency requires and, of course, you will be interviewed before you get a job.

Optical Scan Forms. For a few jobs now and a growing number of jobs in the future, you may be able to complete OPM Form 1203, an optical scan form. This is a quick, easy way for you to answer questions about your qualifications for a certain kind of job. It's also a major boon to the federal agencies. These forms are rated by MARS (Microcomputer-Assisted Rating Services, a system operated by the Office of Personnel Management). The system screens and rates up to 25 applications per minute and can provide immediate ratings to the agency using the service. This system eliminates the labor-intensive, tedious rating process for federal agencies. The Office of Personnel Management is also selling this service to state and local governments, and other organizations. As with the phone system, the service provides a list of eligible applicants. You may have to submit paperwork if the agency takes your name from a register. Sample optical scan questions are at the end of this chapter.

The system screens and rates up to 25 applications per minute.

Federal Job Information Is Online

The Office of Personnel Management is not only automating its application process, it is automating many other federal personnel functions. That means that you, the job seeker, can get application forms and information about federal job vacancies anywhere in the world easier and faster than ever before.

To take a look at these high tech innovations, I visited the government's Model Personnel Office in Crystal City, Virginia. Sponsored by the Office of Personnel Management, the Navy's Human Resources Office and the Defense Civilian Personnel Management Service, this office was established in 1994 as a "reinvention lab" to showcase integrated electronic systems that help federal personnel offices get their work done faster and better. In my visit, I concentrated on the technologies that supply employment information to job applicants.

Here's what I learned. Currently there are three systems that job applicants can use. Each system supplies exactly the same information--worldwide federal job vacancies updated daily by the federal agencies that announce the jobs (Tip: Some agencies may not yet be posting vacancies.) Each system also has a lot of other helpful information. You can access this information in three ways: (1) a touch screen computer found in Federal

Employment Information Centers and some employment offices, (2) the phone in your own home or anywhere else you use a phone, and (3) a personal computer equipped with a modem. Let's look at each of the three systems.

(1) Federal Job Information Touch Screen Computer

Job information doesn't come much easier than on a touch screen computer on what OPM calls a "PC-based kiosk." I found this one very user-friendly. You stand (or in some places you'll sit) in front of the screen and punch colorful, easy-to-read menus, boxes, and maps. You can search for any kind of vacancy, anywhere in the country—or the world. You can also get information on the federal hiring pro-cesses. And if seeing isn't enough, the computer talks to you about key points with its own syn-thetic voice. If you find a job you're interested in, just touch the appropriate box to print the job announcement right off the screen. The printout has the name of a real person to contact (to get the full job announcement), basic qualifying information, and even throws in the hourly and yearly beginning salary on the current pay scale.

As this is written, there are 121 touch screen computers around the country—in each of the Federal Employment Information Centers and in some federal personnel offices and state employment offices. Job seekers from inside and outside the government are welcome to use them. A number of federal organizations are using the touch screen computers for internal merit promotion vacancies.

(2) Career America Connection

Career America Connection is a telephone system, teleservice center, and recruiting message service you can reach by calling (912) 757-3000. It provides current, nationwide information on federal jobs and application procedures, including customized recruiting messages from agencies. The information is available 24 hours a day, 7 days a week. Unlike the touch screen system above, I found this phone system to be very frustrating to use. I tried several calls in the weekend following my visit to the Model Office. However, the Office of Personnel Management says it gets high evaluations on this service from its other customers. If you plan to get information by phone, be sure to have a paper and pencil handy so you can write down the numbers you must punch to access the various categories of information. See the Career America Connection exhibit on the next page.

Career America Connection (912) 757-3000

General Instructions

Punch:

8	repeat any message
9	back up to previous message
0	return to the beginning

Specific Information

1	get employment vacancies
2	order an application form
3	get general information on federal employment, including PMI (Presidential Management Intern program) and other student employment programs

Vacancies   If you punch (1) for employment vacancies, you get the following choices:

1	current vacancies
2	occupations for which applications will be accepted for future vacancies
3	positions advertised by agencies based on urgent needs
4	positions open to current or former federal employees

Forms If you punch (2) to order a form, you get the following choices:

1	PMI application package (You can leave a message with your name, mailing address, and phone number, spelling your last name and street. You will have a chance to listen to your message and make corrections.)
2	summer jobs
3	speak to someone (8 a.m. - 4:30 p.m., ET, Monday - Friday)

For each area you select, you will be led through an additional series of choices. For example, if you select employment vacancies, you will be given numbers that reflect the level (number of years) of your education and experience. You will also be asked to use the key pad to search for either job titles (first three letters) or the job series (numbers). You will also be asked to give the first three letters of the state in which you wish to work.

My first frustration came in not being able to get a response for the District of Columbia. I tried "DIS" and then just "DC." Finally, after I was cut off for giving an incorrect response, I punched "WAS" and I was given a choice of Washington State or Washington, DC.

In several tries, I named a variety of educational and experience levels, job titles and states, but with one exception I was told there were no vacancies. The exception was a GS-9 secretary listing in Washington, DC.

A person who is willing to work in a variety of geographic locations would find it slow going to find vacancies on this system and could run up quite a long distance phone bill at that. The Career America Connection gets about 5,000 calls a week; calls run about 6 minutes each. OPM is planning to make this same job information available in some local areas within the next year or so. Look in the phone book under government listings to find out when this service becomes available in your area.

The Office of Personnel Management also offers federal job Information for the hearing impaired using national and regional TDD (Telephone Device for the Deaf) job hotlines.

**REGIONAL TDD (Telephone Device for the Deaf)
JOB HOTLINE NUMBERS**

Washington, DC:	202-606-0591	Northeastern:	617-565-8913
Southeastern:	919-790-2739	Mountain:	303-969-7047
North Central:	816-426-6022		

Southwestern States:

Arizona	800-223-3131	Louisiana	504-589-4636
New Mexico	505-766-8662	Oklahoma	405-231-4612
Texas	214-767-8115 (Dallas/Ft. Worth)		
Texas	210-805-2401 (other locations)		

Western States:

Alaska	800-770-8973	Nevada	800-326-6868
California	800-735-2929	Oregon	800-526-0661
Hawaii	808-643-8833	Washington	800-833-6388
Idaho	208-334-2100		

(3) Federal Job Opportunities Board

If you've got a modem on your PC, you can access (and download if necessary) federal employment information. Dial (912) 757-3100 for around-the-clock service. This electronic bulletin board is free, but you'll have to register on your first call.

You can view the current federal job announcements on the screen or, in about 5 minutes, you can download the entire list. The FJOB also has a search feature so that you can look for jobs by titles, grades, and series. You'll also find the current salary tables posted on the board, and you can also download the new Optional Form 612.

OPM also sponsors several regional bulletin boards:

Washington, DC Area	(202) 606-4800
Northeastern States	(215) 580-2216
Northcentral States	(313) 226-4423
Western States	(818) 575-6521

Could Agencies Develop Their Own Forms?

The Office of Personnel Management is encouraging federal agencies to use the new federal hiring process, including the optional forms and resumes for applications. However, because the government no longer requires a standard form, federal agencies could, if they choose, develop their own application forms. If agency-specific forms began to proliferate, it would be a huge burden on job hunters who are marketing themselves in a variety of agencies. If agency-specific forms appear, they would probably be for jobs with highly specialized requirements or for use in an electronic application that the agency might develop.

Agencies could also develop their own forms or request the SF-171 for their current employees to use, presumably for promotional opportunities that are not open to the general public. Agencies may also develop computer-compatible versions of the *Optional Application for Federal Employment* and require its use by all applicants.

Agency-specific Questions

Agencies may add any of the following three questions, if applicable, to the information they request from you. These items are unique to certain agencies or positions and are not included on the optional forms.

Spouse Preference. The Department of Defense must give preference in hiring to military spouses. Defense may include the following question in its application materials; for example, in job vacancy announcements or in the *Declaration for Federal Employment*.

Are you applying to exercise Spouse Preference?

( ) Yes ( ) No

If yes, attach a copy of your sponsor's active duty military orders of assignment to the geographic location of the position vacancy or written evidence or documentation that verifies eligibility.

Child Care Workers. By law, applications for federal child care positions contain a question asking whether the individual has ever been arrested for or charged with a crime involving a child and for the disposition of the arrest or charge. Also, the application containing this information must state that it is being signed under penalty of perjury, and identify the penalty. The law requires the hiring agency to obtain the applicant's signed receipt of notice that a criminal record check will be conducted and that the applicant has a right to review and challenge the accuracy of the report. Thus, agencies may add the following question to the *Declaration for Federal Employment* for applicants for child care positions:

Have you ever been arrested for or charged with a crime involving a child? If "Yes," provide the date, explanation of the violation, disposition of the arrest or charge, place of occurrence, and the name and address of the police department or court involved. Note: A Federal agency is required by law to conduct a criminal check. In addition to the purposes explained in blocks 16 and 18, your signature also certifies that (1) your response to this question is made under penalty of perjury, which is punishable by (insert Federal punishment for perjury); and (2) you have received notice that a criminal check will be conducted, of your right to obtain a copy of the criminal history report made available to the employing Federal agency, and of your right to challenge the accuracy and completeness of any information contained in the report.

Indian Child Care Workers. The Departments of the Interior and Health and Human Services may add the following question to the *Declaration for Federal Employment*, for positions that involve regular contact with or control over Indian children:

Have you ever (1) been arrested for or charged with a crime involving a child, and/or (2) been found guilty of, or entered a plea of nolo contendere or guilty to, any offense under Federal, State, or tribal law involving crimes of violence; sexual assault, molestation, exploitation, contact or prostitution; or crimes against persons? If "Yes," provide the date, explanation of the violation, disposition of the arrest or charge, place of occurrence, and the name and address of the police department or court involved. Note: A Federal agency is required by law to conduct a criminal check. In addition to the purposes explained in blocks 16 and 18, your signature also certifies that (1) your response to this question is made under penalty or perjury, which is punishable by (insert Federal punishment for perjury); and (2) you have received notice that a criminal check will be conducted, of your right to obtain a copy of the criminal history report made available to the employing Federal agency, and of your right to challenge the accuracy and completeness of any information contained in the report.

Agencies also have the right to ask any other questions in the initial application if they need this information to evaluate your qualifications and suitability for the targeted job. For example, a few jobs have maximum age requirements. That's why the agency's job announcement is the critical document in the initial application process. That announcement, plus the information requested in the flyer, *Applying for a Federal Job*, should list everything you need to supply in your application for an announced job.

Samples

On the next pages are samples of Optional Form 612, *Application for Federal Employment*; Optional Form 306, *Declaration for Federal Employment*; the flyer, *Applying for a Federal Job*, and Optical Scan Questions for Meteorological Aid.

General Information for Optional Form OF-612

You may apply for most Federal jobs with a resume, this Optional Application for Federal Employment, or other written format. If your resume or application does not provide all the information requested on this form and in the job vacancy announcement, you may lose consideration for a job. Type or print clearly in dark ink. Help speed the selection process by keeping your application brief and sending only the requested information. If essential to attach additional pages, include your name and Social Security Number on each page.

- For information on Federal employment, including job lists, alternative formats for persons with disabilities, and veterans' Preference, call the U.S. Office of Personnel Management at 912-757-3000, TDD 912-744-2299, by computer modem 912-757-3100, or via the Internet (Telnet only) at FJOB.MAIL.OPM.GOV.
- If you served on active duty in the United States Military and were separated under honorable conditions, you may be eligible for veterans' preference. To receive preference if your service began after October 15, 1976, you must have a Campaign Badge, Expeditionary Medal, or a service-connected disability. Veterans preference is not a factor for Senior Executive Service jobs or when competition is limited to status candidates (current or former career or career-conditional Federal employees).
- Most Federal jobs require United States citizenship and also that males over age 18 born after December 31, 1959, be registered with the Selective Service System or have an exemption.
- The law prohibits public officials from appointing. promoting, or recommending their relatives.
- Federal annuitants (military and civilian) may have their salaries or annuities reduced. All employees must pay any valid delinquent debts or the agency may garnish their salary.
- Send your application to the office announcing the vacancy. If you have questions, contact that office.

THE FEDERAL GOVERNMENT IS AN EQUAL OPPORTUNITY EMPLOYER.
PRIVACY ACT AND PUBLIC BURDEN STATEMENTS

■ The Office of Personnel Management and other Federal agencies rate applicants for Federal jobs under the authority of sections 1104, 1302, 3301, 3304, 3320, 3361, 3393, and 3394 of title 5 of the United States Code. We need the information requested in this form and in the associated vacancy announcements to evaluate your qualifications. Other laws require us to ask about citizenship, military service, etc.

■ We request your Social Security Number (SSN) under the authority of Executive Order 9397 in order to keep your records straight; other people may have the same name. As allowed by law or Presidential directive, we use your SSN to seek information about you from employers, schools, banks, and others who know you. Your SSN may also be used in studies and computer matching with other Government file; for example, files on unpaid student loans.

■ If you do not give us your SSN or any other information requested, we cannot process your application, which is the first step in getting a job. Also, incomplete addresses and ZIP Codes will slow processing.

■ We may give information from your records to: training facilities; organizations deciding claims for retirement, insurance, unemployment or health benefits; officials in litigation or administrative proceedings where the Government is a party; law enforcement agencies concerning violations of law or regulation; Federal agencies for statistical reports and studies; officials of labor organizations recognized by law in connection with representing employees; Federal agencies or other sources requesting information for Federal agencies in connection with hiring or retaining, security clearances, security or suitability investigations, classifying jobs, contracting, or issuing licenses, grants, or other benefits; public and private organizations including news media that grant or publicize employee recognition and awards; and the Merit Systems Protection Board, the Office of Special Counsel, the Equal Employment Opportunity Commission, the Federal Labor Relations Authority, the National Archives, the Federal Acquisition Institute, and congressional offices in connection with their official functions.

■ We may also give information from your records to: prospective nonfederal employers concerning tenure of employment, civil service status, length of service, and date and nature of action for separation as shown on personnel action forms of specifically identified individuals; requesting organizations or individuals concerning the home address and other relevant information on those who might have contracted an illness or been exposed to a health hazard; authorized Federal and nonfederal agencies for use in computer matching; spouses or dependent children asking whether the employee has changed from self-and-family to self-only health benefits enrollment; individuals working on a contract, service, grant, cooperative agreement or job for the Federal Government; non-agency members of an agency's performance or other panel; and agency-appointed representatives of employees concerning information issued to the employee about fitness-for-duty or agency-filed disability retirement procedures.

■ We estimate the public reporting burden for the employment information will vary from 20 to 240 minutes with an average of 40 minutes per response, including time for reviewing instructions, searching existing data sources, gathering data, and completing and reviewing the information. You may send comments regarding the burden estimate or any other aspect of the collection of information, including suggestions for reducing this burden, to U.S. Office of Personnel Management, Reports and Forms Management Officer, Washington, DC20415-0001.

■ Send your application to the agency announcing the vacancy.

Form Approved
OMB No. 3206-0219

OPTIONAL APPLICATION FOR FEDERAL EMPLOYMENT - OF 612

You may apply for most jobs with a resume, this form, or other written format. If your resume or application does not provide all the information requested on this form and in the job vacancy announcement, you may lose consideration for a job.

1 Job title in announcement	**2** Grade(s) applying for	**3** Announcement number

4 Last name	First and middle names	**5** Social Security Number

6 Mailing address	**7** Phone numbers (include area code)
	Daytime
City State ZIP Code	Evening

WORK EXPERIENCE

8 Describe your paid and nonpaid work experience related to the job for which you are applying. Do **not** attach job descriptions.

1) Job title (if Federal, include series and grade)

From (MM/YY)	To (MM/YY)	Salary $	per	Hours per week
Employer's name and address				Supervisor's name and phone number

Describe your duties and accomplishments

2) Job title (if Federal, include series and grade)

From (MM/YY)	To (MM/YY)	Salary $	per	Hours per week
Employer's name and address				Supervisor's name and phone number

Describe your duties and accomplishments

9 May we contact your current supervisor?

YES [   ]   NO [   ]▶ If we need to contact your current supervisor before making an offer, we will contact you first.

EDUCATION

10 Mark highest level completed. **Some HS** [   ]   **HS/GED** [   ]   **Associate** [   ]   **Bachelor** [   ]   **Master** [   ]   **Doctoral** [   ]

11 Last high school (HS) or GED school. Give the school's name, city, State, ZIP Code (if known), and year diploma or GED received.

12 Colleges and universities attended. Do **not** attach a copy of your transcript unless requested.

| Name | | | Total Credits Earned | | Major(s) | Degree - Year |
			Semester	Quarter		(if any) Received
1) City	State	ZIP Code				
2)						
3)						

OTHER QUALIFICATIONS

13 **Job-related** training courses (give title and year). **Job-related** skills (other languages, computer software/hardware, tools, machinery, typing speed, etc.). **Job-related** certificates and licenses (current only). **Job-related** honors, awards, and special accomplishments (publications, memberships in professional/honor societies, leadership activities, public speaking, and performance awards). Give dates, but do **not** send documents unless requested.

GENERAL

14 Are you a U.S. citizen?   YES [   ]   NO [   ]▶ Give the country of your citizenship. _____

15 Do you claim veterans' preference? **NO** [   ]   **YES** [   ]▶ Mark your claim of 5 or 10 points below.
5 points [   ]▶ Attach your DD 214 or other proof. **10 points** [   ]▶ Attach an *Application for 10-Point Veterans' Preference* (SF 15) and proof required.

16 Were you ever a Federal civilian employee?
NO [   ]   YES [   ]▶ For highest civilian grade give:

Series	Grade	From (MM/YY)	To (MM/YY)

17 Are you eligible for reinstatement based on career or career-conditional Federal status?
NO [   ]   YES [   ]▶ If requested, attach SF 50 proof.

APPLICANT CERTIFICATION

18 **I certify** that, to the best of my knowledge and belief, all of the information on and attached to this application is true, correct, complete and made in good faith. **I understand** that false or fraudulent information on or attached to this application may be grounds for not hiring me or for firing me after I begin work, and may be punishable by fine or imprisonment. **I understand** that any information I give may be investigated.

SIGNATURE   **DATE SIGNED**

☆ U.S. GPO:1994-383-912/09047

Declaration for Federal Employment Instructions

The information collected on this form is used to determine your acceptability for Federal employment and your enrollment status in a Life Insurance program. You may be asked to complete this form at any time during the hiring process. Follow instructions that the agency provides. If you are selected, you will be asked to update your responses on this form and on other materials submitted during the application process and then to recertify that your answers are true before you are appointed.

Your Social Security Number is needed to keep our records accurate, because people may have the same name and birth date. Executive Order 9397 also asks Federal agencies to use this number to help identify individuals in agency records. Giving us your SSN or any other information is voluntary. However, if you do not give us your SSN or any other information requested, we cannot process your application. Incomplete addresses and ZIP Codes may also slow processing.

You must answer all questions truthfully and completely. A false statement on any part of this declaration or attached forms or sheets may be grounds for not hiring you, or for firing you after you begin work. Also, you may be punished by fine or imprisonment (U.S. Code, title 18, section 1001).

Either type your responses to this form or print clearly in dark ink. If you need additional space, attach letter-size sheets (8.5" x I I"), including your name, Social Security Number, and item number on each sheet. It is recommended that you keep a photocopy of your completed form for your records.

The Office of Personnel Management is authorized to request this information under sections 1302, 3301, 3304, and 8716 of title 5 of the U.S. Code. Section 1104 of title 5 allows the Office of Personnel Management to delegate personnel management functions to other Federal agencies. If necessary, and usually in conjunction with another form or forms, this form may be used in conducting an investigation to determine your suitability or your ability to hold a security clearance, and it may be disclosed to authorized officials making similar, subsequent determinations.

Public burden reporting for this collection of information is estimated to vary from 5 to 30 minutes with an average of 15 minutes per response, including time for reviewing instructions, searching existing data sources, gathering the data needed, and completing and reviewing the collection of information. Send comments regarding the burden estimate or any other aspect of the collection of information, including suggestions for reducing this burden, to Reports and Forms Management Officer, U.S. Office of Personnel Management, 1900 E Street, N.W., Washington, D.C. 20415.

ROUTINE USES: Any disclosure of this record or information in this record is in accordance with routine uses found in System Notice OPM/GOVT-1, General Personnel Records. This system allows disclosure of information to training facilities; organizations deciding claims for retirement insurance, unemployment, or health benefits; officials in litigation or administrative proceeding where the Government is a party; law enforcement agencies concerning a violation of law or regulation; Federal agencies for statistical reports and studies; officials of labor organizations recognized by law in connection with representing employees; Federal agencies or other sources requesting information for Federal agencies in connection with hiring or retaining, security clearance, security or suitability investigations, classifying jobs, contracting, or issuing licenses, grants, or other benefits; public and private organizations, including news media, which grant or publicize employee recognition and awards; the Merit Systems Protection Board, the Office of Special Counsel, the Equal Employment Opportunity Commission, the Federal Labor Relations Authority, the National Archives, the Federal Acquisitions Institute, and Congressional offices in connection with their official functions; prospective non-Federal employers concerning tenure of employment, civil service status, length of service, and the date and nature of action for separation as shown on the SF 50 (.or authorized exception) of a specifically identified individual; requesting organizations or individuals concerning the home address and other relevant information on those who might have contracted an illness or been exposed to a health hazard; authorized Federal and non-Federal agencies for use in computer matching; spouses or dependent children asking whether the employee has changed from a self-and-family to a self-only health benefits enrollment; individuals working on a. contract, service, grant, cooperative agreement or job for the Federal government; non-agency members of an agency's performance - or other panel; and agency appointed representatives of employees concerning information issued to the employee about fitness-for- **duty** or agency-riled disability retirement procedures.

Optional Form 306
September 1994
U.S. Office of Personnel
Management

Declaration for Federal Employment

Form Approved:
O.M.B. No. 3206-0182
NSN 7540-01-368-7775
50306-101

GENERAL INFORMATION

1 FULL NAME

▶

2 SOCIAL SECURITY NUMBER

▶

3 PLACE OF BIRTH (Include City and State or Country)

▶

4 DATE OF BIRTH (MM/DD/YY)

▶

5 OTHER NAMES EVER USED (For example, maiden name, nickname, etc.)

▶

▶

6 PHONE NUMBERS (Include Area Codes)

DAY ▶

NIGHT ▶

MILITARY SERVICE

	Yes	No
7 Have you served in the United States Military Service? *If your only active duty was training in the Reserves or National Guard, answer "NO".*		

If you answered "YES", list the branch, dates (MM/DD/YY), and type of discharge for all active duty military service.

BRANCH	FROM	TO	TYPE OF DISCHARGE

BACKGROUND INFORMATION

For all questions, provide all additional requested information under item 15 or on attached sheets. The circumstances of each event you list will be considered. However, in most cases you can still be considered for Federal jobs.

For questions 8, 9, and 10, your answers should include convictions resulting from a plea of nolo contendere *(no contest)*, but omit (1) traffic fines of $300 or less, (2) any violation of law committed before your 16th birthday, (3) any violation of law committed before your 18th birthday if finally decided in juvenile court or under a Youth Offender law, (4) any conviction set aside under the Federal Youth Corrections Act or similar State law, and (5) any conviction whose record was expunged under Federal or State law.

	Yes	No
8 During the last 10 years, have you been convicted, been imprisoned, been on probation, or been on parole? (Includes felonies, firearms or explosives violations, misdemeanors, and all other offenses.) *If "Yes", use item 15 to provide the date, explanation of the violation, place of occurrence, and the name and address of the police department or court involved.*		
9 Have you been convicted by a military court-martial in the past 10 years? (If no military service, answer "NO".) *If "Yes", use item 15 to provide the date, explanation of the violation, place of occurrence, and the name and address of the military authority or court involved.*		
10 Are you now under charges for any violation of law? *If "Yes", use item 15 to provide the date, explanation of the violation, place of occurrence, and the name and address of the police department or court involved.*		
11 During the last 5 years, were you fired from any job for any reason, did you quit after being told that you would be fired, did you leave any job by mutual agreement because of specific problems, or were you debarred from Federal employment by the Office of Personnel Management? *If "Yes", use item 15 to provide the date, an explanation of the problem and reason for leaving, and the employer's name and address.*		
12 Are you delinquent on any Federal debt? (Includes delinquencies arising from Federal taxes, loans, overpayment of benefits, and other debts to the U.S. Government, plus defaults of Federally guaranteed or insured loans such as student and home mortgage loans.) *If "Yes", use item 15 to provide the type, length, and amount of the delinquency or default, and steps that you are taking to correct the error or repay the debt.*		

ADDITIONAL QUESTIONS

	Yes	No
13 Do any of your relatives work for the agency or organization to which you are submitting this form? (Includes father, mother, husband, wife, son, daughter, brother, sister, uncle, aunt, first cousin, nephew, niece, father-in-law, mother-in-law, son-in-law, daughter-in-law, brother-in-law, sister-in-law, stepfather, stepmother, stepson, stepdaughter, stepbrother, stepsister, half brother, and half sister.) *If "Yes", use item 15 to provide the name, relationship, and the Department, Agency, or Branch of the Armed Forces for which your relative works.*		
14 Do you receive, or have you ever applied for, retirement pay, pension, or other pay based on military, Federal civilian, or District of Columbia Government service?		

CONTINUATION SPACE / AGENCY OPTIONAL QUESTIONS

15   Provide details requested in items 8 through 13 and 17c in the continuation space below or on attached sheets. Be sure to identify attached sheets with your name, Social Security Number, and item number, and to include ZIP Codes in all addresses. If any questions are printed below, please answer as instructed (these questions are specific to your position, and your agency is authorized to ask them).

CERTIFICATIONS / ADDITIONAL QUESTION

APPLICANT: If you are applying for a position and have not yet been selected. Carefully review your answers on this form and any attached sheets. When this form and all attached materials are accurate, complete item 16/16a.

APPOINTEE: If you are being appointed. Carefully review your answers on this form and any attached sheets, including any other application materials that your agency has attached to this form. If any information requires correction to be accurate as of the date you are signing, make changes on this form or the attachments and/or provide updated information on additional sheets, initialing and dating all changes and additions. When this form and all attached materials are accurate, complete item 16/16b and answer item 17.

16 I certify that, to the best of my knowledge and belief, all of the information on and attached to this Declaration for Federal Employment, including any attached application materials, is true, correct, complete, and made in good faith. I understand that a false or fraudulent answer to any question on any part of this declaration or its attachments may be grounds for not hiring me, or for firing me after I begin work, and may be punishable by fine or imprisonment. I understand that any information I give may be investigated for purposes of determining eligibility for Federal employment as allowed by law or Presidential order. I consent to the release of information about my ability and fitness for Federal employment by *employers, schools, law enforcement agencies*, and *other individuals and organizations* to *investigators, personnel specialists*, and *other authorized employees of the Federal Government*. I understand that for financial or lending institutions, medical institutions, hospitals, health care professionals, and some other sources of information, a separate specific release may be needed, and I may be contacted for such a release at a later date.

16a   Applicant's Signature ▶
          (Sign in ink)   Date ▶

16b   Appointee's Signature ▶   Date ▶ | APPOINTING OFFICER: Enter Date of Appointment or Conversion ▶
          (Sign in ink)

17 **Appointee Only** *(Respond only if you have been employed by the Federal Government before):* Your elections of life insurance during previous Federal employment may affect your eligibility for life insurance during your new appointment. These questions are asked to help your personnel office make a correct determination.

	Date (MM/DD/YY)		
17a When did you leave your last Federal job?			
	Yes	No	Don't Know
17b When you worked for the Federal Government the last time, did you waive Basic Life Insurance or any type of optional life insurance? ·			
17c If you answered "Yes" to item 17b, did you later cancel the waiver(s)? *If your answer to item 17c is "No," use item 15 to identify the type(s) of insurance for which waivers were not cancelled.* ·			

United States Office of Personnel Management

OF 510
(September 1994)

VETERANS' PREFERENCE IN HIRING

❑ If you served on active duty in the United States Military and were separated under honorable conditions, you may be eligible for veterans' preference. To receive preference if your service began after October 15, 1976, you must have a Campaign Badge, Expeditionary Medal, or a service-connected disability. For further details, call OPM at **912-757-3000**. Select "Federal Employment Topics" and then "Veterans." Or, dial our electronic bulletin board at **912-757-3100**.

❑ Veterans' preference is not a factor for Senior Executive Service jobs or when competition is limited to status candidates (current or former Federal career or career-conditional employees).

❑ To claim 5-point veterans' preference, attach a copy of your DD-214, *Certificate of Release or Discharge from Active Duty*, or other proof of eligibility.

❑ To claim 10-point veterans' preference, attach an SF 15, *Application for 10-Point Veterans' Preference*, plus the proof required by that form.

OTHER IMPORTANT INFORMATION

❑ Before hiring, an agency will ask you to complete a *Declaration for Federal Employment* to determine your suitability for Federal employment and to authorize a background investigation. The agency will also ask you to sign and certify the accuracy of all the information in your application. **If you make a false statement in any part of your application, you may not be hired; you may be fired after you begin work; or you may be fined or jailed.**

❑ If you are a male over age 18 who was born after December 31, 1959, you must have registered with the Selective Service System (or have an exemption) to be eligible for a Federal job.

❑ The law prohibits public officials from appointing, promoting, or recommending their relatives.

❑ Federal annuitants (military and civilian) may have their salaries or annuities reduced. All employees must pay any valid delinquent debts or the agency may garnish their salary.

APPLYING FOR A FEDERAL JOB

In addition to information requested in the job vacancy announcement your application or resume **MUST contain** the following information:[1]

JOB INFORMATION

❑ Announcement number, title and grade(s) of the job for which you are applying.

PERSONAL INFORMATION

❑ Full name, mailing address *(with Zip Code)* and day and evening phone numbers.

❑ Social Security Number

❑ Country of citizenship *(Most Federal jobs require United States citizenship.)*

❑ Veterans' Preference

✔ If you served on active duty in the United States Military and were separated under honorable conditions, you may be eligible for veterans' preference. To receive preference if your service began after October 15, 1976, you must have a Campaign Badge, Expeditionary Medal, ora service-connected disability. For further details, call OPM at 912-757-3000. Select "Federal Employment Topics" and then "Veterans." Or, dial OPM's electronic bulletin board at 912-757-3100. A computer and modem is required.

✔ Veterans' preference is not a factor for Senior Executive Service Jobs or when competition is limited to status candidates *(current former Federal career or career-conditional employees).*

✔ To claim 5-point veterans' preference, attach a copy of your DD-214, *Certificate of Release or Discharge from Active Duty,* or other proof of eligibility.

✔ To claim 10-point veterans' preference, attach an SF-15, *Application for 10-Point Veterans' Preference,* plus the proof required by that form.

❑ Reinstatement eligibility *(If requested, former federal employees must attach a SF-50, proof of your career or career-conditional status.)*

✔ Highest Federal grade held *(Also give job series and dates held.)*

---

[1] Reprinted from OPM brochure *Applying For a Federal Job*, OF 510 (September 1994)

EDUCATION

❑ High School

  ✔ Name, city, and state *(Zip Code if known)*
  ✔ Date of diploma or GED

❑ Colleges and universities

  ✔ Name, city, and state *(Zip Code if known)*
  ✔ Majors
  ✔ Type and year of any degrees received *(If no degree, show total credits earned and indicate whether semester or quarter hours.)*

❑ Send a copy of your college transcript only if the job vacancy announcement requests it.

WORK EXPERIENCE

❑ Give the following information for your paid and nonpaid work experience related to the job for which you are applying. *(Do not send job descriptions.)*

  ✔ Job title *(include series and grade if federal job)*
  ✔ Duties and accomplishments
  ✔ Employer's name and address
  ✔ Supervisor's name and phone number
  ✔ Starting and ending dates (month and year)
  ✔ Hours per week
  ✔ Salary

❑ Indicate if we may contact your current supervisor.

OTHER QUALIFICATION

❑ **Job-related** training courses *(title and year)*
❑ **Job-related** skills; for example, other languages, computer software/hardware, tools, machinery, typing speed.
❑ **Job-related** certificates and licenses *(current only)*
❑ **Job-related** honors, awards, and special accomplishments; for example, publications, memberships in professional or honor societies, leadership activities, public speaking, and performance awards *(Give dates but do not send documents unless requested.)*

Sample Questions for Optical Scan Form

GS-1341

FORM APPROVED
OMB NO. 3206-0036

NAME:_____   SSN: _____

United States Office of Personnel Management
Honolulu Service Center
300 Ala Moana Blvd.
Box 50028
Honolulu, Hi 96850

Supplemental Qualifications Statement

for

METEOROLOGICAL AID

Occupation Code: 1341C

INSTRUCTIONS

In this booklet you will be asked a number of questions concerning the above occupation. Please answer all questions to the best of your ability. Mark your responses in Section 17 (Occupational Questions) of the Qualification and Availability Form (Form C). Return the Form C and any additional forms requested to our office at the address listed above.

The answers you provide to the questions in this booklet will be verified by us against the information you provide in other application forms and by checking the references you have provided or will provide to us. Any exaggeration of your experience or any attempts to conceal information can result in your being removed from a Federal job and in barring you from seeking Federal employment in the future.

For further information concerning other Federal employment opportunities you may contact any State Employment Service Office.

We appreciate your interest in Federal employment.

OPM FORM 1170   FH-9130 (6/93)

GS-1341   2

SUPPLEMENTAL QUALIFICATIONS STATEMENT
FOR
METEOROLOGICAL AID (OCCUPATION CODE: 1341 C)

1. <u>SELECT</u> THE ONE STATEMENT BELOW WHICH BEST DESCRIBES YOUR HIGHEST LEVEL OF EDUCATION OR EXPERIENCE. DARKEN THE OVAL CORRESPONDING TO THAT STATEMENT IN SECTION 17 ON FORM C.

A. I do not have any work experience.
B. I have held a job for at least three months that involved following specific instructions.
C. I have held a job for at least six months which required following instructions, keeping records or making calculations.
D. I am a high school graduate or have the equivalent, i.e. GED.
E. I have at least one year of education above high school which included at least one course in meteorology, mathematics, engineering, or physical science.

For each task in the following group, choose the statement from the list below that best describes your experience and/or training. Darken the oval corresponding to that statement in Section 17 on Form C. Please select only one letter for each item.

A - Yes   B - No

2. I have taken at least two high school mathematics courses.
3. I have taken at least two high school science courses.
4. I have passed high school mathematics courses with at least a B average.
5. I have graduated from high school with an overall average of at least a B.
6. I have averaged grades of C or below in most high school classes.
7. I have completed at least one year of education above high school with at least a B average.
8. I have taken at least two mathematics courses above the high school level.
9. 1 have passed college level mathematics courses with at least a B average.

For each task in the following group, choose the statement from the list below that best describes your experience and/or training. Darken the oval corresponding to that statement in Section 17 on Form C. Please select only one letter for each item.

A - YES   B - NO

GS-1341   3

10.   I have passed college level science courses with at least a B average.
11.   I have passed college level courses with an overall average of at least a B.
12.   My jobs involved counting money or cash register work.
13.   My jobs involved tabulation of data or numbers.
14.   My jobs do not involve using mathematics or keeping records.
15.   My jobs required that I follow specific written or oral instruction.
16.   My jobs required that I keep records by recording information or data.
17.   My jobs do not require me to keep records.
18.   I always ask for approval to take time off from work.
19.   My supervisors have commended me for good work.
20.   My supervisor sometimes reprimands me for my attendance or work.
21.   I have through education, experience or hobby, measured temperature.
22.   I have through education, experience or hobby, measured air movement.
23.   I have through education, experience or hobby, measured air density.
25.   I have through education, experience or hobby, measured cloud types.
26.   I have through education, experience or hobby, recorded or coded data.
27.   I have through education, experience or hobby, prepared messages for transmission.
28.   I have through education, experience or hobby, extracted information from written messages.

OPM FORM 1170   FH-9130 (6/93)

RATINGS

104.0	082.0	095.0
103.0	090.0	095.0
094.0	089.0	095.0
092.0	087.0	095.0
097.0	ID	092.0
096.0	091.0	090.0
089.0	089.0	086.0
ID	079.0	084.0
063.0	ID	099.0
081.0	103.0	099.o
099.0	103.0	087.0
099.0	093.0	085.0
086.0	092.0	100.0
085.0	098.0	100.0
081.0	098.0	096.0
ID	099.0	096.0
084.0	099.0	

Chapter Four
Step-by-Step Instructions
for the New Optional Application Form 612

In this chapter, you'll learn how to format and write the new *Optional Application for Federal Employment* (OF 612). Your application will be customized to fit a specific job that an agency has announced and you have targeted.

The Optional Form is just two folded pages—18 questions in all. It also has a short tear-off page with general instructions and admonitions. Compared to the old *Standard Form 171 Application for Federal Employment* (four pages, 49 items), it sounds like a piece of cake.

Unfortunately it isn't. Yes, the application form is improved, but much of the content is the same as the old form. It's still going to take time and thought to present yourself and your qualifications in such a way that someone will want to hire you instead of the dozens, or in some cases hundreds, of others who are competing for the job.

The new Optional Form 612 asks the hard stuff about your experience, training, skills and accomplishments. These are the questions that take the most time and thought. The good news, however, is that the government is only looking for information that is directly *related* to the job you're applying for. In the old form, you had to catalog every job you had for the past 10 years, all your training whether it was needed for the job you're applying for, and all your awards and special qualifications. The new Optional Form advises you to customize your application to specific jobs. You provide only the information that fits each job you want, based on the requirements listed in the job announcement. This means that personnel officials and hiring authorities don't have to wade through stuff that is not relevant to the job they have announced.

The bad news is, however, that you have to supply addresses, salaries and supervisors for all jobs you list, even those that are several years old. This is just like the old form and it's time-consuming to construct this information. The company may have moved and your former supervisors may be in other jobs (and you don't know their current phone numbers). I

Yes, the application form is improved, but much of the content is the same as the old form.

wish the new form innovators had deferred getting this much detail until later in the hiring process.

Where Do You Get Optional Form 612?

You will get a copy of Optional Form 612 and other application information when you request a job announcement from the personnel office of a federal agency. You may also get a copy at a Federal Employment Information Center or state employment office, or you may call OPM's automated telephone system at (912) 757-3000 or by TDD at (912) 744-2299. A copy of the form is in Chapter 3. The Office of Personnel Management has also put the form online for you to read or download. If you have a computer with a modem, dial the Federal Job Opportunities Board, (912) 757-3100.

Your best bet is commercial software, the *Quick and Easy Federal Jobs Kit*. You'll get a form that can be expanded or reduced expertly to fit your exact qualifications. The software gives tips from Dennis V. Damp's sixth edition of *The Book of U.S. Government Jobs*. You can also get a search feature to make sure you've used powerful buzz words that reviewers are looking for. The software also includes the companion form, *Declaration for Federal Employment*, as well as resume formats in case you choose to use a resume as your application.

You also have the option of using any PC software to prepare the application, but you are responsible for making sure that your application contains all the information requested in the flyer, *Applying for a Federal Job*, and in the job announcement.

The Form You Present

Before we begin the question-by-question instructions, I'd like for you to examine the form as it's printed and visualize what you want the final product to be, along with any supplementary forms or attachments.

Unless you just got out of school and have hardly any work or volunteer experience—or unless you're applying for a job that is so hard to fill that the government is desperate for applicants—forget the thought that you can apply with two short pages and that's it. If you use the Optional Form, the application package you present for the job you've targeted may include several documents:

- Your principal document is the Optional Form prepared by typing, word processing, or using commercial software like the *Quick and Easy Federal Job Application Kit*. The advantage of using this software is that you can expand the space to describe your experience,

training and skills and keep the information flowing as organized on the form without cumbersome attachment sheets. Attachment sheets are a pain for the reviewer. It means flipping from questions on a front sheet to continuation of the response on attachment sheets. You'll also find sample expanded pages following the Appendices of this book. If you don't have the software, be sure to copy and use these expanded pages.

The Office of Personnel Management considers the two-page form the minimum space for describing your qualifications. Limiting yourself to two pages is not smart unless you have few job-related qualifications, such as recent graduates or applicants for entry or wage grade positions. Even then, with the tips in this book everyone should be able to do more to highlight their qualifications based on the requirements in the job announcement. You may or may not include a short cover resume. See Chapter 6.

*A*ttachment sheets are a pain for the reviewer.

- Your package may also include a supplemental qualifications statement. Prepare this statement to respond to the specific qualifications described in the job announcement as special rating factors. These factors have different names, but are often called "Knowledge, Skills, Abilities and Other Characteristics (KSAOs)." You may avoid preparing this attachment only if you have fully customized the Optional Form around the rating factors. Sometimes an agency provides you with a supplemental qualifications form as part of the application package it sends out. **Although it may be presented as an option, it really isn't**. Complete the form. See Chapter 5 for assistance. (Note: The term, "Supplemental Qualifications Statement," is also used for optical scan questionnaires.)

- Some announcements require you to attach college transcripts, special forms (like those to indicate status and veterans' preference), and other information. Do not include these attachments unless they are required.

*K*eep good records of your career.

- Often an agency will send you a voluntary applicant background survey with questions about your race, sex, age, disability, and national origin. It is for statistical purposes only and does not affect your individual application.

You'll find a check list for your final package in Chapter 8.

Preliminary Steps

Here are the preliminary steps to preparing your application.

- Keep good records of your career. If you don't have a system, start one now. Keep a lifetime career file with diplomas, certificates, personnel actions, awards and recognition, evaluations, notes from other people praising your work, personal summaries or outlines of responsibilities and accomplishments, work samples, old resumes and application forms, etc. Some people have a shoe box in a closet; others have a desk drawer; others have elaborate personal filing systems. It doesn't matter how it looks, just so you always have career information at your fingertips. You need to draw on this information many times for future applications and resumes, so don't neglect to keep these records.

- Keep a supply of high-quality bond paper (white, ivory, cream or other neutral colors) for printing and/or photocopying your final application. Also have on hand a supply of envelopes large enough to mail or deliver your application without folding it. Folding an application into a small business envelope creates a creased disaster.

- Skim the Optional Form 612 so you will be familiar with the information requested.

- Read the agency job announcement and the flyer, *Applying for a Federal Job*, carefully. Some agencies will attach the flyer to the announcement; other agencies may put information from the flyer in the job announcement. Information from the form is in Chapter Three. Underline or use a yellow high lighter to mark the information you will need to transfer to the form and the qualifications—including special rating factors—that you must emphasize on the form.

Page One of the Optional Form 612

Job Title Sought and Personal Information (Questions 1 - 7)

1 and 2. Job Title and Grade(s) Applying For

Fill in the job title listed in the announcement. Grade is the level of difficulty. (Each grade requires a certain number of years of experience

and/or training. See Chapter 2. If the job announcement specifies several grades (for example 9/12), indicate only the highest grade(s) you are interested in or believe you are qualified for. If you aren't sure what grade you're qualified for, put in the entire range indicated on the announcement. EXAMPLE: Program Analyst, GS-343-11/12

3. Announcement Number

Fill in the number on the job announcement.

4-7. Full Name, SSN, Mailing Address, and Phone Number

Fill in every blank exactly. If your legal name is not the name by which you are commonly known, add your "everyday" name in parentheses following your legal name. EXAMPLE: Evans, Decatur John (Jack)

Work Experience

8. Describe your paid and nonpaid work experience related to the job for which you are applying.

Don't rush through this part of the application. Lots of people are qualified for the job you want. The way you describe your salaried, volunteer, and other experience may mean the difference between being "qualified" and "highly qualified," as determined by government reviewers. I recommend that you spend as many hours as it takes to organize, write and edit the experience blocks.

Don't rush through this part of the application.

The Optional Form provides you with blocks for two jobs, but you may need more space to describe your accomplishments in these jobs. Also, you may have more than two jobs or other experience that relate to the job you've targeted. You are not confined to the space provided on the form. You may add more blocks and expand or reduce these blocks to the size you need to market your experience and skills. You'll find ready-to-use expanded blocks after the Appendices.

Re-read the job announcement, paying special attention to what kind of and how much experience is required. Look for the special skills or evaluation factors that are sought. You should emphasize the experience you have that relates to this job.

Organize Your Experience

Whether you're using a resume, the Optional Form, or the government's old Standard Form 171, you should organize all your experience—paid and volunteer—on a worksheet. This worksheet will help you:

• Decide what experience to put in and what to throw out based on the qualifications announced for a specific job.

● Determine the sequence of your experience. That is, decide which positions to describe first, second, etc. on the form (or resume). For most people, a reverse chronological sequence will probably be best and would cause government evaluators less confusion since they are used to this sequence. Start with your current or more recent experience and work backward, selecting only those jobs or volunteer activities that relate to the targeted job. Today, however, the applicant gets to chose the best way to present his or her qualifications. If your most powerful, appealing qualifications are not in your current or most recent job, then chose the sequence that works best to showcase your talents. In other words, you may present your best experience first, but understand that this may confuse the reviewer.

As a general guide, organize all experience for the last 10 years—and longer if your experience relates to the job areas you believe you're qualified for. Here's a sample worksheet from a person who is applying for a position as an accountant.

Sample Experience Worksheet

Targeted Job: Accountant, GS-510, 5/7
Agency and Job Announcement Number:

EXPERIENCE	DATES	RELATES TO JOB	NOTES
Jr. Accountant (Smith and Evans, CPA)	July 1994-present	Yes	Need half page. Show as job 1.
Treasurer, National Honor Society (local chapter)	Sept. 1992-June 1994	Yes	Volunteer—took about 2 hours a week. Computerized chapter's financial records using Quicken. Need a half page. Show as job 2.
Camp Counselor	summers, 1991, 92, 93	No	
drug store clerk, evenings and weekends	20 hrs. a week, Sept. 1990-June 1992	Partly—backed up accountant as a records clerk about 25 percent of time	Need half page. Show as job 3. Emphasize skills in dBase, Lotus 1-2-3.

What Kind of Nonpaid Work Experience Counts?

Every kind of volunteer or nonpaid work experience has the potential for giving you the opportunity to demonstrate specific or generic skills for targeted jobs. Here are some examples:

- Officer of a community, school, home owners, church, philanthropic, honorary, trade, or professional organization.
- Leader, chair, or active member of a committee or team in any organization.
- Work in a school office or lab as a volunteer or on a scholarship.
- Volunteer for a hotline, hospital, Head Start center, shelter for the homeless, or retirement home.
- Organizer, coordinator or active participant in special projects, theatrical events, or fund raisers.
- Member of land use groups, community clean-up projects, or environmental task forces.
- Editor, reporter, writer, business manager or other position on a school or organizational publication.

Like salaried jobs, these and many other activities give you the opportunity to exercise responsibility, demonstrate skills, and achieve goals. Although the application asks for experience which is "relevant" to the job, certain skills transfer readily from one area to another. These skills include planning, evaluating, coordinating, monitoring, communicating, working in teams, and many others.

For non-salaried experience, provide complete information about the number of hours you worked and for how long, or your experience will not be credited. The *Qualifications Standards* distinguish between general and specialized experience, but both count. See Chapter 2. Suppose you have been a volunteer fireman, experience that appears to have nothing to do with your targeted job of a public information specialist. However, you did considerable community education and fund raising in your work for the volunteer fire department. If you describe your responsibilities and accomplishments in community education, this experience may count as general experience because it offered a general background of work skills suitable for the broad area of work expected of a public information specialist. Depending on the requirements of the announcement, this may be counted as specialized experience.

Tips for Completing Each Experience Block

After you have organized and analyzed your work experience, you are ready to complete the experience blocks on the Optional Form. Here are some tips for the basic information on each job:

Job Title (if federal, include series and grade)—It is not unusual, especially in government, to have a title on paper that is different from or more descriptive of your actual job. Use the title that best matches the job you're applying for. If necessary, use both. EXAMPLE: Chief, Audit Branch, Division of Administration (Budget Analyst 560, GS 13)

From/To—Provide the month and year you started and ended the position. A good format is "7/94." For your current job, you have worked to the "present." If you only worked for a short time in the job, include the exact day. For example, if you worked from 6/30/94 to 8/1/94, you worked only about a month, and reviewers need to know this in order to credit your experience properly.

Salary and Hours Per Week—As a general guide, give your annual salary. If your compensation included housing or other perks, add the annual value to the figure. EXAMPLE: *$55,000 per year (includes housing)*. For most professionals, the practice is to put *40 plus* hours even though you are not compensated for extra time. If you regularly work longer hours and are compensated for this time, put something like *40 plus about 10 hours overtime*.

Employer's Name and Address—Include the full address of the organization that employed you. If the company or agency has moved, gone out of business, or the address is not available, put the name, city, and state as in a resume. If you work for a large organization, put the address that has your personnel records, especially if the job is not recent. For example, if you teach school, put the City or County Board of Education as your employer with the name of the school in parenthesis. Or, you could lead with the name of the school followed by the name and address of the board.

Supervisor's Name and Phone Number—Usually the name and phone number of a current or recent supervisor is available, and you will have no trouble providing it. The more time passes, however, the less likely you can supply a working phone number for a previous supervisor. In this case, put the person's name and add *number unavailable*. If the person is deceased, indicate this fact.

Tips for Formatting Your Duties and Accomplishments

Aim for a clean, well-organized, clearly-written, concise narrative that invites reading. See the samples at the end of this chapter. Here are some formatting tips.

- **Break up your narrative into short, snappy chunks.** Use short sentences, short paragraphs, bullets, and ample white space for increased readability.

- **Use upper and lower case for your narrative, not all caps.** Upper case (CAPS) is hard to read. You may use all caps for short headings, however.

- **Organize and describe your experience under headings and subheadings.** Here is a sample group of headings and the kind of information under heading:

  Responsibilities—Tell broad areas of work you are responsible for, including the scope (where your office is located, the mission of your unit related to the mission of your parent organization, how you fit in).

  Duties—List day-to-day tasks and activities (Keep this short unless you attach accomplishments to them. Unadorned, this stuff reads too much like a job description.)

  Accomplishments—Give the results of what you've done either as an individual or as part of a team. Emphasize accomplishments above all else. *Recruited and trained 100 day care volunteers* (an accomplishment) is better than *Responsible for the recruitment and training of volunteers* (a responsibility) or *Recruit and train volunteers* (a duty).

  Skills—Describe your abilities, aptitudes, knowledge, work habits, and ways of working and relating to people.

  Another way to organize your narrative is to use the quality ranking factors from the job announcement. For example, one factor might be "Demonstrated organizational skills with an emphasis on coordination of activities within a specific area of specialty." A heading could be *Organizational and Coordination Skills*. Under such a heading you might describe your work in coordinating satellite broadcasts and workshops for a national conference.

Tips for Writing Your Duties and Accomplishments

- **Use your own words**. Don't copy your own job descriptions word-for-word and don't attach them to your 171.

- **Use simple, direct sentences**. Show clearly what you accomplished in each position.

- **Use strong words**. The strongest words are verbs, but there are other powerful nouns and phrases like *organizational change, reinventing government, reengineering, benchmarking,* and *employee involvement*. The savvy federal job hunter should be alert to this vocabulary for the 90s and use these words liberally in the job application. See Chapter 7. Also use or paraphrase key words from the job announcement, provided you back up these words with specific examples and accomplishments. If you can't, you may not be qualified for the position.

- **Write in the active voice**. Active voice tells who took the action described in the verb—you! *I negotiated and handled the entire office furniture procurement in just two months.* (active voice) is better than *The entire office furniture procurement was negotiated and handled in just two months.* (passive voice).

- **Avoid jargon unless you explain it**. Use language appropriate to your field, but write so that anyone can understand what you do.

- **Use "I" sparingly**. If you use bullets, leave out "I" (first person) and begin with the verb. The voice is active; the "I" is implied. EXAMPLE: *Wrote marketing training material for more than 100 field staff.*

- **Use parallel structure**. That is, express similar ideas in similar ways. For example, in this bulleted list, I begin each item with a verb. If I had decided to begin with a noun, this item would read *"Parallel Structure."* The next bullet would read *"Quotes."*

- **Quote people**. Include brief excerpts of what people say or write about your work. Sparingly used, this is an excellent way to sprinkle in good words from people who know you well. Example: The senior advisor commented, "The speech you wrote for the Commissioner was perfect for the occasion."

- **Give details**. Tell who, what, when, where, how much, how often, and with what results. What projects did you initiate and/or direct? What teams did you lead or actively participate in? How much money did you or your team save your company or agency? What processes did you improve? What bureaucratic barriers did you remove? How many customers did you serve and with what level of satisfaction? How many programs do you administer? What size budget do you administer? What have you done to reduce costs? What are your personal and organizational outcomes and how do you measure them? How many phone calls do you answer in a day? Who is calling and what kind of information do they want? What kind of reports did you write and what resulted? How many reports have you stopped writing because you surveyed and found that your audience didn't need them anymore?

  Evidence of personal accomplishments is important, even if the accomplishments are minor. You are trying to show that you made a contribution rather than just followed a routine, no matter what the level of the job. EXAMPLE: *Arranged four local office relocations in FY 1995, coordinating timely move of more than 2,000 employees and furniture and equipment worth about $3 million.* See the sample experience blocks at the end of this chapter.

- **Show how much time you spend in an activity if your title isn't clear**. If your work contains more than one kind of activity—such as personnel and budget—give the approximate percentage of time for each. You may put the percentages in parentheses after the description of the activity. Don't do this unless it's important to the targeted job. For example, you work as a staff assistant and have duties in both budgeting and personnel. You are aiming for a job in personnel, so highlight your personnel duties and provide the percentage of time that you spend in this activity. Made sure everything adds up to 100 percent.

- **Don't abbreviate words, and don't use acronyms unless you write the full name the first time**. Example: *Metro Area Rapid Transit Authority (MARTA)*.

- **Summarize**. If you expand the experience block to a full page, and have amply demonstrated the experience that qualifies you for the targeted job, you may wish to summarize your knowledge, skills or special abilities that relate to the announced job. Example:

  - Detailed knowledge of technologies involved in air, land or naval warfare or mobility.
  - In-depth understanding of the Department of Defense Planning, Programming and Budgeting System (PPBS).
  - Ability to prepare complex, detailed management reports and studies on a wide range of issues and topics.
  - Skill in presenting and defending conclusions and recommendations; ability to persuade management to accept ideas and conclusions.

Before and After Experience Sample

One of the most common mistakes that federal job applicants make is using the exact words of their job description to describe their qualifications. These are the same duties and responsibilities that anyone in the same position would have. To make things worse, they often format the words as one never-ending paragraph in very small type. This doesn't tell the rater or manager anything. When I want to hire someone, I screen applications like this out fast. Here's an example taken from a GS-12 management analyst's actual application:

Before

Performs studies and analyses of new and existing procedures or proposals for standard use throughout Customer Support. Studies consist of a wide variety of complex issues that the Service is co-responsible for with the user for implementation of ADP support. Includes planning for and the utilization of resources, statistical measurements of productivity, work distribution, management surveys, organizational make-up, cost data and all other requirements in carrying out the Service's responsibilities. Establish and maintain contact with various organizational elements to gather data for use in the study analysis. Prepares long-range plans and objectives and provides supporting documentation on the issues requested. Issues are difficult to define and seldom will past procedures or standard procedures be applicable as the application usually requires an evolving system subject to new innovations, new equipment and ever changing policies. Serves a source of technical information and data to assist the Director with completing correspondence and inquiries by providing cost data, and analysis of Service operations. Uses available data to develop logical and sound recommendations to the Director on organizational activities and responsibilities. Assists the Director with the accomplishment of Service responsibilities by coordinating and providing liaison with the analysts of any and all internal Service requirements including planning, budget, travel, and provides measurements of productivity, work distribution, management surveys, organizational make-up, cost data and all other requirements in carrying out the Service's responsibilities. Assists the Director in developing and implementing the Customer Support Program/Operating Budget Plans. Assists in the development and implementation of appropriate performance standards for Customer Support staff. In this capacity deals with other organizational divisions. Participates in the development of divisional Project Management Policy and Procedures relating to internal operations. Assures that assigned projects conform to applicable policies and documentation standards.

After (Here's what the applicant might have written:)

SCOPE OF RESPONSIBILITY

Worked as one of six management analysts on a small customer support unit of 22 people that did work force surveys, analyzed agency productivity and work distribution, and helped agency managers forecast and plan personnel and training needs. My responsibilities also included planning, budget and travel to meet the internal needs of our unit.

DUTIES AND ACCOMPLISHMENTS

- SURVEY EXPERT—Served as survey expert on cross-agency team that developed and implemented an agency-wide employee satisfaction survey that reached more than 6,000 people. I developed and revised the survey questionnaire with assistance and suggestions from team members. I worked with the procurement office to contract with the company that analyzed and tabulated the results based on requirements that I developed. Our agency is using the survey results to make improvements in our employee suggestion program and our employee rewards and recognition system.

- PEER RECOGNITION—Following the above survey, researched recognition systems in private and public organizations. Wrote the administrative procedures to implement peer recognition system in our agency.

- TEAM EVALUATIONS—Worked as a member of a small unit team that developed team evaluations to supplement individual performance appraisals—an effort that has improved morale, provided quicker feedback and improved our unit's effectiveness.

- On my own initiative, I studied the Government Performance and Results Act of 1993 before its passage. This research helped our unit, and therefore our agency, get a head up on implementing the act even before the Office of Management and Budget issued guidance for the Executive Branch.

Page Two of the Optional Form 612

9. May we contact your current supervisor?

Answer *no* unless your have discussed your interest in other employment with your supervisor.

10-12. Education

The questions on education appear straight forward. Answer as directed and fill in completely, including all zip codes. You may need to expand the space needed to respond, depending on how many schools you attended and the requirements in the job announcement.

If you are currently working on a degree that you expect to complete within the next year, indicate the year and add "EXPECTED" next to the year. EXAMPLE: B.A., 1996 (EXPECTED). If you did not receive a degree, you may attach a list of courses that relate to the announced job. Include the number and semester or quarter hours.

You will not need to submit transcripts for most jobs. However, some technical positions—such as computer specialist—may require a transcript or a list of courses. The job announcement will tell you to send a transcript if it is needed.

13. Other Qualifications

The categories under Other Qualifications call for training, skills, licenses, honors, awards and special accomplishments *as they relate to the job you've targeted.* Many federal job applicants list everything they've ever learned or experienced, whether or not these activities relate to the kind of job they are applying for. To compound the problem, they often attach photocopies of every certificate, every congratulatory letter, and every news clipping in their career. It is hard for an evaluator (who is giving you a rating) or a program manager (who will hire you from the list of qualified candidates) to plow through a paper mountain. Keep your application as crisp and concise as possible; unnecessary information could harm your chances. The point is you don't want to slow the reviewers down or risk a resentment, however latent. Look at it as a chance to demonstrate your efficiency. You want to give the reviewers polished gems, not a mine field they have to work.

Nevertheless, unless you're just entering the job market, the space provided on the form is not enough to do justice to this category of job qualifications. Several rating points will likely be allotted to this section, and you don't want to lose these points. Expand this space as needed to do justice to your qualifications.

Job-related training

These tips should help:

- Begin with the most recent training and list in reverse chrono-logical order unless you have a clear reason to do otherwise. A good reason would be to put the best stuff first.

- Provide only the title of the training and year as directed in the instructions. I also recommend that you indicate how many days or hours for each course or seminar. Do not attach certificates.

- Include all kinds of training: in-service training, workshops, seminars, professional conferences devoted to training, private study, correspondence courses, and distance learning training (computer-based or by satellite broadcasts).

- If you have a lot of different kinds of relevant training, group by categories, such as computer training, communications, cultural diversity, and marketing.

- Include generic or cross-functional skills training. These kinds of skills are useful in a variety of positions, especially as government flattens its hierarchies and focuses more on improving its service to the public. Examples are: teamwork, leadership, communications, public speaking, writing, negotiating, supervision, quality management, reengineering, customer service, project management, and software applications such as word processing, graphics, databases and spreadsheets.

- Include self-study. It is valuable information for a hiring official, even if you don't get any points from a personnel specialist or a rating panel. For example, many people are studying from the plethora of resources on quality management and organizational change. They have read books by successful practitioners, visited companies or agencies that practice quality management or have won quality awards, listened to quality experts on audio tapes while they commute, and watched videotapes in their own homes. Log this kind of activity and summarize it in your application as job-related self study. Other fields lend themselves to self-study, especially software applications. If you got a manual and taught yourself PageMaker or Harvard Graphics or PowerPoint, then include it. Note it as self-study, and show by title, year, and number of hours you spent.

- Use common sense to tell you if certain training is relevant to the announced job, but if you are not sure, put it in.

Job-related Skills

This is a catch-all question, designed for you to throw in things that didn't fit anywhere else. Despite its miscellaneous nature, this question is important; some types of responses can give you rating points. Here are the examples on the form with some tips about each category:

Computer Software/Hardware and Other Technologies—List your competencies. Computer skills are valuable today for everyone from executives to clericals. Some computer skills are expected for almost any managerial, professional, technical, or support position in the government, even if this qualification is not listed on the job announcement. Even the Senior Executive Service Job Bulletin advises applicants to describe their computer skills.

Tools and Machinery—List competencies that are required by or related to the announced job. These will usually be obvious, such as operating or using printing presses, medical equipment, surveying instruments, high speed mail sorters, and traffic control instruments. Give model numbers or other descriptors as appropriate.

Other Languages—Given the growing cultural and linguistic diversity in America today, proficiency in other languages is important even if this factor is not stated on a job announcement. List your linguistic skills, including the level of your proficiency EXAMPLES: *conversational Japanese; fluency in Spanish; moderate reading and speaking in French*, etc.)

Typing Speed—Do not list this skill for a professional or technical position unless it is mentioned as a requirement on the job announcement. However, *Keyboard Proficiency* is critical for many jobs in today's computer-dominated work environment, so mention it.

Current Licenses—List only licenses, including dates and licensing authority (such as a state), that relate to or are required by the job. For example, a real estate license for a realty specialist.

Job-Related Honors, Awards and Special Accomplishments (publications, memberships in professional/honorary societies, leadership activities, public speaking and performance awards)—List and give dates, but do not attach copies. Here are tips:

Honors, awards, fellowships

- List performance awards, service awards, citations, certificates, quality step increases, certificates of appreciation, letters of appreciation or commendation, cash awards, scholarships, fellowships, and other honors or recognition for job performance, scholarship, or service.

- Include awards from work, school, church, community, and professional organizations if they demonstrate relevant skills or qualifying factors mentioned in the job announcement.

- Organize these honors in reverse chronological order unless you have an important award that deserves top billing. Give the year of the honor and the reason for the recognition if this is not evident. If you have a lot of honors, group them in some logical way (school, work, community, for example).

- Don't list honors that are unrelated to the targeted job, such as a neighborhood swim trophy if you are applying for a job as a management analyst. However, if you have won national or international athletic competitions, you may include them because they show unusual motivation, stamina, and perseverance.

Publications

- List titles and dates of all publications that you wrote or edited, no matter how insignificant they may seem to you. Publications include reports, guides, handbooks, instructions, and pamphlets. Even if you only wrote and photocopied 25 copies of a "how to" manual for hospital volunteers, that is writing experience.

- If appropriate, add a sentence or phrase about the significance of the publication or the size of the distribution. Example: *the first government-wide publication on this subject.*

- List all titles and writing examples, even if you mentioned them in the experience blocks. However, if you are a writer with many publications to your credit, you may wish to list only your primary publications and tell how many other publications you have by subject, not by title.

Memberships in Professional/Honor Societies

- List relevant professional, civic and scholarly affiliations, past and present (in reverse chronological order by year). If your involvement in an organization is extensive and related to the targeted job, then also describe your activities in an experience block as discussed in question 8.

- Join a professional organization right now if you don't already belong. Professionals are expected to belong to professional organizations to stay current in their field and to make contacts that will help on the job.

Leadership Activities

- List and date in reverse chronological order any offices or leadership roles that you have held in any organization (school, community, home owners, church, political, etc.). If your involvement in any organization is extensive, also describe in an experience block as discussed in question 8.

- List any involvement in teams or committees as either a leader or an active, contributing member.

- Use some sensitivity in mentioning political or religious activities. These involvements could work for or against you in the eyes of a hiring authority. Discrimination is illegal, but human beings have biases even if they don't acknowledge them. Consider these elements in your job search strategy on a job-by-job basis.

Public Speaking

You don't have to be a polished speaker to have speaking experience. Here are some tips:

- List any experience in which you taught, persuaded, or briefed an audience. Consider presentations to clubs, workshops, committees, classes, Sunday school, and Toastmasters.

- If you are an accomplished and frequent speaker, list your major presentations in recent years at seminars and conferences. Emphasize topics that relate to the qualifications in the job announcement.

- Summarize some of your public speaking activities. For example: *Gave 20 presentations on "New Techniques in Dental Hygiene" as guest lecturer at Woodward Community College, 1994 - present.*

Hobbies

Include information about hobbies if they relate to your targeted job. For example, a person aiming for a position as an audio-visual specialist might include: *Maintain and catalog personal collection of more than 1,000 books, films, tapes, and CDs on mammals. Lend or show to interested groups on request.*

14. Are you a U.S. citizen?

Answer yes or no; if no, give country of citizenship. Generally speaking, you must be a citizen to get a federal job.

15. Do you claim Veterans' Preference?

Answer yes or no. Veterans' Preference is the special consideration given to qualified veterans. Generally, you will get five points added to your application evaluation rating if you were honorably discharged. Ten points are added if you are disabled, and in some cases if you are the spouse, widow, widower, or mother of a disabled veteran. If you claim 5 points, attach your DD 214 or other proof. If you claim 10 points, attach an Application for 10-Point Veterans' Preference (SF 15) and proof required.

16. Were you ever a federal civilian employee?

Answer yes or no. For highest civilian grade, give the job series number, the grade level and the dates you held that grade. Example: *GS 334* (series), *11* (grade), *1/91 - 10/94* (from, to). As a reminder to federal employees: The question asks for "highest," not current or last grade.

17. Are you eligible for reinstatement (based on career or career-conditional federal status)?

Answer yes or no. If yes, attach Standard Form 50 as proof only if the announcement requires it. "Status" means you are currently in a federal civilian job, or you formerly held a federal job and you may be reinstated or rehired without competing again. "Career-conditional" is the initial appointment to a federal job in the competitive service. It leads to a permanent or "career" position after 3 years of satisfactory service.

Look carefully at the job announcement. It indicates whether the job is open only to candidates with status or is open to anyone else. However, sometimes the word "status" isn't used. For example, if the "area of consideration" is "nationwide," the job is open to both status and non-status applicants.

If you aren't sure, ask the federal personnel specialist whose name and phone number are on the job announcement.

18. Applicant Certification

Read the certification. Sign and date in ink, and submit the page with the original signature (not a photocopy) to the personnel office. (Note: Certification is not required at this stage of the process if you submit a resume or a SF-171.) The date must be after the date the job is announced and by or before the closing date. If you are responding to several similar job announcements, make photocopies or print additional copies from your computer printer before you sign each application. Some offices will accept a faxed application and allow the applicant to sign another copy later. Don't fax without asking.

Experience Samples

Most of the experience samples on the following pages are from real people, but many dates and identifying factors were changed. A few samples were made up to illustrate a variety of jobs.

Accountant

2) Job title: Accountant/Assistant to the General Manager

From 2/1/90 To 4/1/93 Salary $42,000 per yr.   *Hours per week* 40

Employer's name & address   *Supervisor's name &*
Acme Insulating Company, Inc.   *phone number*
888 Riverdale Road   John Davis
Riverdale, MD 00000   (301) 000-0000

BACKGROUND

Entered as Accountant for rapidly-growing small business whose annual gross tripled in three years to $8 million. Assumed concurrent duties as Assistant to the General Manager nine months after joining firm, with managerial functions that required 30% of my time. Developed understanding of the principles of energy conservation and the techniques of home and industrial insulation.

DUTIES AND ACCOMPLISHMENTS

- Maintained company books, with full responsibility for accounts payable and receivable, payroll, taxes and general fiscal administration.
- Set up annual budget, established regular cash flow analysis, and provided company with first accurate financial statements in its 5-year history.
- Led small team that researched and initiated the computerization of several accounting functions, including payroll, holding costs down to 1989 level, although company volume had tripled and continued to grow. Studied system which supplied full management information; supervised conversion to the new system.
- Initiated in-house auditing procedures.
- As Accountant, hired, trained, and supervised two junior accountants. As Special Assistant to the General Manager, indirectly oversaw the work of twenty administrative, sales, and clerical staff.
- Assisted General Manager in developing contract bidding policy.
- Developed comprehensive marketing study with assessment of competing companies as first step in expanding services into four-county area.
- Prepared management advisory reports. Participated actively in the development of company vision, goals and objectives, and strategic plan.
- Simplified forms for travel and expense accounts, cutting administrative costs by 10 percent.

Excerpt from letter of commendation from Company President at time of large salary increase in 1992: "Thanks to you, we are able to see where we've been, but more important, where we are going. You provide an invaluable service to the company. We're glad you are part of our team."

Materiel Management Specialist

3) Job title: Materiel Management Monitor
From 9/6/87 To 4/1/89 Salary $32,000 per yr.   *Hours per week* 40

Employer's name & address   *Supervisor's name &*
Renshaw Transportation Center   *phone number*
10905 Ritchie Highway   Warren C. Coe
Glen Burnie, MD 29228   (301) 000-0000

RESPONSIBILITIES

Managed and monitored the total operations for management of documentation, equipment, material, and supplies for export shipment. Was responsible for over $2 million in equipment and material. Used process improvement techniques and quality management principles to direct a modernization program to improve logistics, supply management systems, shipping, purchasing procedures, and policies for this supply house managed by a subcontracting company.

DUTIES AND ACCOMPLISHMENTS

- Supervised five employees located at a subcontractor warehouse and five company employees. Was responsible for all warehousing and case management activities.
- Directed the smooth flow of supplies for depots/vendors to the subcontractor.
- Received a cash bonus and commendation for my accomplishments in establishing systems and controls for documentation, accounting, and reporting.
- Set up and led company/subcontractor employee team that evaluated and improved on warehouse subcontractor services in terms for shipping services and packaging.
- Monitored compliance with regulations when shipping hazardous or restricted cargo.
- Made decisions concerning action required for damaged or shortage of supplies, equipment, or materials. Reviewed carrier bills of lading and received documents.
- Directed effective movement of all material. Determined appropriate shipping procedures, i.e. air to surface; diverting shipping from surface to air.

AREAS OF KNOWLEDGE AND SKILL

- Examining, evaluating and devising improved systems for management of property.
- Applying numerous federal export-import rules and regulations concerning supply systems and inventory management.
- Directing distribution and storage management operations.
- Overseeing and improving packaging and shipping techniques.
- Supervising staff: motivating, training, planning and assigning projects; presenting organization goals.
- Studying workflow, devising more efficient procedures.

Health Care Analyst

4) Job title: Health Care Analyst
From 1/1/89 *To* 3/1/91 *Salary* $42,725 *per* yr.

Hours per week 40 plus

Employer's name & address
XXXXX County Health Foundation, Inc.
1910 Sunset Avenue
xxxx, FL 00000

Supervisor's name &
phone number
Amy Renfrow
(000) 000-0000

DUTIES AND RESPONSIBILITIES

Served as Health Care Analyst on a three-member monitoring team for the local desig-nated professional standards review organization for a variety of health care and medical facilities, with greatest concentration in area of services paid with public funds.

ACHIEVEMENTS

- Monitored and analyzed the quality of health care for ten area hospitals, three psychiatric clinics, and three nursing homes for the elderly, through preliminary evaluation which preceded review. With team, documented quality and level of health care, costs, admitting practices, and other factors.
- Served as team leader in more than half the reviews conducted in the past year. Directed team in establishing goals, setting work priorities, collecting and analyzing a wide variety of data, and reporting to committees of physicians and other health professionals organized for the purpose of peer review. Provided full staff back-up for review.
- Advised committees on apparent adherence to standards, as well as deficiencies and deviations. Recommended in-service training and seminars on quality management customer service for four facilities to improve services and correct deficiencies in patient care. The Foundation accepted and implemented these recommendations.
- Maintained contact with Medicare and Medicaid payment groups, also established and maintained liaison with similar review organizations in the metropolitan area.
- Developed, on own initiative, a comprehensive cost function analysis of all area hospitals which was used as the basis of a local newspaper series. This series led to numerous reforms in local hospitals and other hospitals in the state.
- Designed a patient-care assessment form now used by all review teams.
- Suggested major change in professional standards relating to the use of health care paraprofessionals that led to official revision in the standards manual.

SKILLS SUMMARY

- Ability to establish and maintain effective relationship with working associates.
- Ability to communicate with people at all levels.
- Strong skill in analyzing complex health-related functions.
- Ability to plan and organize work.

Volunteer

1) Job title: Volunteer
From 6/15/90 *To* present   *Salary* N/A   *Hours per week* 20 plus

Employer's name & address   *Supervisor's name &*
Broadview Service Foundation, Inc.   *phone number*
810 Silver Street   N/A - Vince Kinlow is Founda-
Valdosta, GA 00000   tion Pres. #(000) 000-0000

Serve as member of the Broadview Service Foundation, a non-profit organization that responds to local community needs in a large but relatively sparsely populated county. Served as member of the policy-making Board of Directors since January 10, 1994; chaired two committees as noted below.

ACHIEVEMENTS

Transportation Committee (Feb. 1990 - present)

Chaired committee that initiated in-depth study of transportation needs in a rural county that had no public transportation system. Developed a demographic analysis of residential areas, business centers, educational and cultural institutions, health and medical facilities, and other areas. Persuaded County Commission to hold public hearings in several areas of the county. Developed alternative public and private transportation proposals. Organized lobbying campaign to convince Commission to fund limited public transportation system using vans purchased with revenue sharing funds. As supplement to program, initiated a five-county Volunteer Transportation Corps to provide transportation to essential services for elderly, handicapped, ill, or low income persons. Currently serve as consultant-advisor to other counties. Appointed by County Commissioner to seven-county regional planning organization in March 1994; at present serve on Commission's Transportation Subcommittee.

Day Care Committee (Aug. 1990 - Jan. 1993)

Co-chaired committee that organized day care facilities in five community churches. Made initial survey with team; developed community awareness campaign; recruited volunteers and coordinated campaign which raised $100,000 in cash and in kind. Negotiated with Regional Community Care, Inc., to take over two of the facilities which were then converted to Head Start Centers under Health and Human Services guidelines. Currently serve as member of advisory committee on fund raising for three other facilities which remain day care centers for the children of low and moderate income families. The programs are funded on sliding-pay scales, plus public and church contributions.

AWARDS: Chamber of Commerce Citizen of the Year, 1993; Community Service Award from Foundation, 1992.

Law Enforcement Officer

2) Job title: Supervisory Federal Officer, GS-12, 083
From 8/18/89 *To* 7/1/91   *Salary* $38,537 *per* yr.   *Hours per week* 40 plus

Employer's name & address   *Supervisor's name & phone*
Federal Protective Service   *number*
Police Division   Mary Lou Warren
Fort Meade, MD 00000   (301) 000-0000

Supervised federal officers assigned to Fort G.G. Meade and the National Security Agency complex including federal areas of responsibility and control at the Baltimore/Washington Airport complex in Baltimore. Responsible for training and coaching staff, with emphasis on newly assigned personnel.

DUTIES AND RESPONSIBILITIES

- Directed personnel in the investigation of sensitive security matters and crimes against persons and property.
- Scheduled assignments, special details, and patrol vehicles for up to fifty federal officers.
- Led a team that developed and implemented many new scheduling techniques to improve mission coverage. Received Special Act award for my leadership.
- Directed traffic enforcement units.
- Directed personnel in emergency situations such as fire, disturbances, medical emergencies, and bomb threats, including search and disposal.
- Trained staff in developing suspects, interviews and probable cause for further action if necessary.
- Coordinated efforts with high ranking officials, local authorities and the U.S. Attorney's Office to plan mutual guidelines concerning terrorist activity, suspected criminal and security violations, including espionage and sabotage and violations of the rules and regulations.
- Developed an excellent working rapport with local police jurisdictions, the U.S. Attorney's Office and Magistrate's Court, leading to ways to collaborate on mutual endeavors.
- Wrote concise, factual, well-received status reports, and trained staff to write clear, accurate reports.
- Had Secret Clearance with access to special intelligence (TSSI).

SKILLS SUMMARY

- Supervising, scheduling, and coordinating law enforcement officers and activities.
- Assigning cases, reviewing performance, editing reports, and ensuring all aspects are handled within established agency guidelines.
- Developing and maintaining excellent relationships with other law enforcement agencies.
- Training and developing responsible, career-oriented staff; motivating and ensuring top performance.

Inventory Management Supervisor

5) *Job title:* Inventory Management Supervisor, MS/E8

From 9/11/82 *To* 2/1/83   *Salary* $3,723 *per* month   *Hours per week* 40 plus

Employer's name and address   *Supervisor's name and phone*
200th Theater Army Materiel Mgt. Center   *number*
Aircraft Troop Support Division   Anthony Randolph
APO New York 09052   (000) 000-0000

Supervised six inventory managers responsible for managing all power generation equipment within the Aircraft/Troop Support System Division. Directed the transformation of a previously loosely-controlled, complex item management section into a highly-coordinated, effective group of managers with an efficient management and control system.

- Redistributed and disposed of excess generators throughout the theater.
- Upgraded the stocks.
- Resolved many logistical problems and handled numerous crisis management situations requiring wartime logistical problem solving.
- Served as the Standard Army Integrated Logistics System Coordinator, interfacing the materiel distribution for management of major end items at the wholesale level with the continental U.S. Army European retail materiel readiness centers, and the level materiel management centers in the U.S. Army Depots and contractor facilities.
- Supervised inventory managers who were responsible for equipment valued at over $3.5 million.

ACCOMPLISHMENTS
- Established a float factor for USAREUR units by coordinating usage factor with CONUS Readiness Command.
- Established turn-in procedure for unserviceables being returned to depot and/or CONUS, cutting costs by 15 percent.
- Supervised and coordinated the return, on yearly basis, of 128 unserviceable engines for repair and return to U.S. Army customers worldwide; saved the army $753,792 by returning these engines.
- Established TARP for unserviceable engines, attained a sustained supply position, thus eliminating costly shipping and handling charges for the movement of engines between CONUS and USAREUR.
- Maintained constant liaison with Reserve Storage Activity (RSA) personnel between accounting, storage, issue, and shipment activities.
- Established excellent safety level in order to sustain customer demands and prevent zero balance of assets, while avoiding excess position of assets.
- Received numerous letters of appreciation for contributions to the U.S. Army Europe's overall mission and accomplishments.

Computer Assistant

5) Job title: Computer Assistant, 335 Series GS 9
From 9/11/87 *To* 2/1/89   *Salary* $28,288 *per* year   *Hours per week* 40 plus

Employer's name & address   *Supervisor's name & phone*
NASA/Goddard Space Flight Center   *number*
Greenbelt, MD 20771   Sara K. Mason
                                                        (301) 000-0000

SCOPE OF RESPONSIBILITIES

My responsibilities were extensive and varied, and involved much more than the title "Computer Assistant" implies. As an administrative assistant, I became highly involved in making decisions, analyzing, coordinating, and managing projects and programs. These include major purchasing of computer systems/local area networks, managing a multi-million dollar inventory, directing conventions and meetings, developing and trouble-shooting computer systems and programs, and creating management reports.

COMPUTERS

- Participated in the evaluation of computer-based information management and office automation systems, both hardware and software, for the Division. Worked with Division management and computer specialist to develop requirements and design programs for programs such as: resources, budgets, manpower and financial report-ing, project management, and calendar management.
- Have in-depth knowledge of two data base management systems involving two computers with different operating systems. Used the computers and management systems to design and redesign programs for business, financial, and management reports. These reports provided information in structured formats for use in tracking resources by staff personnel.
- Ordered computer terminals for the division and branches plus furniture and accessories exceeding $10,000. Negotiated and handled entire procurement proce-dures, including preparation of technical specifications and evaluations of technical proposals by vendors.
- Served as the Office Automation Specialist for the staff. Participated in application programming, served as liaison with computer firms, evaluated software for changing program and report requirements, and troubleshot the entire system for both program and equipment problems.
- Used ORACLE on the VAX 780 and RAMIS II on the IBM 4341 for writing reports and programs such as space utilization, travel, manpower plans, and budgets.

PROCUREMENT / PROPERTY MANAGEMENT

- Managed the purchase, inventory record-keeping, and movement of over $8 million in equipment, including six high-tech computer systems. Successfully passed a special audit by NASA Headquarters of property as a result of high control and efficient record-keeping.

LOGISTICS

- Developed an extensive Space Utilization Report for the movement of the Division to new offices and facilities. Developed a facility reorganization plan, including floor plans, environmental decisions, and design. Developed complete management report.
- Served as move coordinator for the relocation of the new Division, including directing the redistribution of furnishings and personnel. Coordinated all telephone and computer installations and movement of large equipment. Worked with tight deadlines with no major problems.

PERSONNEL

- Sponsored and trained three Puerto Rican students for the Institute for Computer Applications Program for two summers.
- Directed the Division participation in the Summer High School Apprentice Research Program (SHARP) serving as mentor and sponsor for high school youths in a research apprenticeship program (1987, 1988).
- Successfully managed the Combined Federal Campaign for the division for ten years - always achieving outstanding participation in the Division and Directorate. Skilled in gaining volunteer cooperation in all aspects of the program.
- Chairman, Affirmative Action Employment Management Advisory Committee one year. Served as staff liaison to top management. Researched discrimination complaints, made recommendations, and wrote reports.
- Active in Federally Employed Women's Programs, Prince George's Chapter - three years. Served as Newsletter Editor, President, Secretary and Chairman of Legislative Committee at various times.

SYMPOSIA / MEETING MANAGEMENT

- Served as the Conference Coordinator for a summer-long program sponsored cooperatively by NASA, University of Maryland, and the American Electrical Engineering Society. This full-time, five-month project involved handling all logistics, accommodations and meeting planning for a Fellowship program attended by 30 full-time Fellows and representatives of the scientific and research industry. Scheduled, planned, publicized and prepared materials for ongoing meeting seminars within the Division.

Note to reader: This experience, taken from an older SF-171, contains information that would be relevant to several kinds of positions. If this applicant were applying today for a position as a computer specialist, she might eliminate the parts headed Logistics, Personnel, Symposia/Meeting Management and focus only on Computers and Procurement/Property Management (which dealt with computer procurements). If she were applying for the job of Supervisory Computer Specialist, she would use all of the headings, perhaps adapting words from the rating factors in the job announcement. She should shorten the write-up to one page or less because she held this job several years ago and it is probably less important as her career has progressed.

Secretary

1) Job title: Secretary, GS-318-7
From 9/11/90 *To* present   *Salary* $28,288 *per* year   *Hours per week* 40 plus

Employer's name & address
Center for XXXXXX
XXXXXX Division
123 Midway Court
Atlanta, GA 30308

Supervisor's name & phone number
Angela Warren, MD
(412) 000-0000

RESPONSIBILITIES

Serve as Secretary to the Director of the Office of Health Policy Development. Act as lead clerical among seven clerical staff. Control all office correspondence and action items from meetings and memoranda. Also prepare requests for travel and travel vouchers for about 30 professional staff.

DUTIES AND ACCOMPLISHMENTS

- Prepare reports, statistical charts, budgets, memoranda, briefing materials, slides, and other documents using WordPerfect 6.0 for Windows, PowerPoint, and several graphics software programs. I excel in document design and simple computer graphics. I key about half of the narrative documents and receive the other half from analysts via a local area network (LAN). I develop many of the graphics, including tables, graphs and pie charts, from the analysts' hand-drawn sketches.

- Developed the specifications for an automated correspondence control system in consultation with office analysts and managers. **Received a Special Act Award for this work, which went far beyond my job description.**

- Receive, control and assign about 25 memoranda and action items weekly. Determine priorities in conjunction with the Deputy Director; return items more appropriately handled in other offices; prepare responses to inquiries of a general nature (about six per month) for the signature of the Director and the Deputy Director.

- Arrange and coordinate up to 10 meetings or conferences each month and two general meetings a year with members of the medical community.

- Receive more than 25 phone calls daily, some of a sensitive nature involving contagious diseases requiring immediate referrals or action. Demonstrate poise and ability to communicate with people at all levels.

- Maintain a comprehensive electronic directory of office staff to which I added, on my own initiative, phone numbers and addresses of frequently-contacted staff from other offices in the region, Washington, D.C., and health care providers or administrators.

- Served on a regional team that studied internal customers needs and improved our work process. Twelve suggestions have been implemented, cutting down on some bureaucratic controls and improving our effectiveness.

Mid-Level Manager

2) Job title: Director, Office of Instructions
From 9/1/88 *To* 6/30/91   *Salary* $69,023 *per* year   *Hours per week* 40 plus

Employer's name & address   *Supervisor's name & phone*
XXXXXXXXX Administration   *number*
6986 Pennsylvania Ave., NW   Cynthia W. Gwinn
Washington, DC 00000   (000) 000-0000

SCOPE OF RESPONSIBILITY

Administered the office that edits and produces instructions for the Agency's 1400 field offices and other operational components and that leads the effort to improve the 240 million notices sent to the public each year. Managed a $2.3 million printing budget and the work of a GM-15 deputy, three GM-14 managers, three GM-13 project leaders and one GS-12 supervisor who in turn oversaw the work of more than 65 analysts and other staff, GS-4 to GM-14. Chaired a monthly meeting of GS/GM 13-15 representatives of divisions whose authors wrote the instructions. Our office edited and produced 40,000 camera-ready pages for initial printing, resulting in more than 250 million pages of instructions distributed nationwide. We also improved the formatting and language of dozens of kinds of letters affecting millions of beneficiaries and taxpayers.

ACCOMPLISHMENTS

Here are examples of activities that streamlined production, saved money, improved the quality of the instructions, and/or improved user satisfaction:

PROCESS IMPROVEMENTS AND COST SAVINGS

-   Initiated and directed ongoing effort that replace outdated, unreliable publishing (typesetting) system based on computer mainframe with software that runs on microcomputers, thereby reducing processing time and cutting costs. Accomplishments included moving 30,000-page instructions database from a mainframe to a mini-computer, installing postscript printers, and purchasing a customized microcomputer-based version of typesetting software.

-   Wrote proposal and decision memo for Commissioner to deliver Agency instructions on CD-ROM. Played major role in briefing Commissioner, who approved a pilot that led to national implementation after I left the agency. CD-ROM saved the Agency at least $14 million in 5 years, including reducing the workload of maintaining a massive paper system. It also ensure consistent, timely instructions nationwide.

CONTINUED

Job 2, CONTINUED   First Name, Middle Initial, Last Name, SS# 000-00-000

- Initiated and directed effort to streamline inefficient, wasteful instructions distribution system, a project that saved considerable money and improved service. For example, we stopped distributing thousands of pages of instructions to users who only needed a few hundred pages. Another reform brought about an interface between the time and attendance system with the instructions distribution system, eliminating need for manual adjustments as staff levels change.

- Initiated and directed ongoing initiative to improve management information, including office's first budget monitoring system and first computerized system to track and report on status of about 400 instructional transmittals annually.

- Initiated successful effort to move $7 million forms printing budget out of our office, an initiative which cut out an unnecessary bureaucratic layer and speeded-up forms printing process.

PRODUCT QUALITY

- Introduced revised editorial standards to improve the quality of the instructions and directed a 9-month effort to rewrite and clear a new Writers' Handbook for the Agency's 800 instructions authors. Also introduced a larger, contemporary typeface to increase readability of instructions.

USER SATISFACTION

- Oversaw series of visits to hundreds of workers in a variety of sites who use program instructions. We listened to their needs and used their ideas for improvements to initiate projects to improve content and to seek approval to pilot CD-ROM technology as a delivery mechanism.

STAFF DEVELOPMENT

- Initiated and conducted seminars on career development for both lower and upper graded staff to improve their chances in competing for promotions.

- As funds permitted, sought and procured training in writing, editing, manual production, document design, software applications, analysis, negotiation, human relations, management, communications and other areas to increase staff skill levels and improve published products.

- Worked with my managers and classification specialists to upgrade several positions that had been changed by technology or higher standards for work performed.

Student

1) Job title: Accounting Claims Auditor
From 6/1/94 *To* 8/30/94   *Salary* $1,000 *per* month   *Hours per week* 40

Employer's name & address   *Supervisor's name &*
Lake Haven Paper Company   *phone number*
8990 Fantasy Lane   Angela Rodriguez
Lake Haven, PA 00000   (000) 000-0000

- Created, prepared and audited claims filed by customers and sales representatives.
- Served as member of team that managed $100 million in accounts receivable and $220 million in office accounts payable.
- Investigated billing discrepancies between accounts payable and vendors.

---

2) Job title: Human Resources Clerk
From 6/1/93 *To* 8/30/93   *Salary* $960 *per* month   *Hours per week* 40

Employer's name and address   *Supervisor's name and*
Craven's Department Store   *phone number*
583 Main Street   Martin Salzberg
Morton, PA 00000   (000) 000-0000

- Created and maintained personnel database for more than 120 employees.
- Wrote routine memos about leave, store hours and other administrative matters.
- Checked references on job applications; assisted Regional Human Resources Manager in hiring and firing procedures.

---

3) Job title: Student Assistant
From 9/1/91 *To* 5/30/95   *Salary* $120 *per* week   *Hours per week* 20
    (except for summer months)
Employer's name and address   *Supervisor's name*
Admissions Office   *and phone number*
Farmingham College   Dean Anna S. Smith
Lovely Lake, NY 00000   (000) 000-0000

- Maintained 4,000 student files on DBASE IV (only student with access to student data)
- Handled registration and conducted campus tours.
- Compiled student statistical data and assisted in preparing federal grant application packages.

Sample Student Exploratory Cover Letter

115 Halpern Avenue
Apt. 108
Hamilton, NY 14850
May 1, 1994

Ms. Agnes Weathersby, Chief
Financial Services Division
Office of XXXXXXXX
330 Independence Ave., SW
Washington, DC 20003

Dear Ms. Weathersby:

I'm writing at the suggestion of James Bolling, PhD, who served with you last year on a public/private sector task force on international fund transfers. Dr. Bolling, who was my teacher in International Studies at Colgate University, said that you may soon have openings for auditors and budget analysts in your division.

As you can see from the enclosed resume, I will graduate in June from the Johnson Graduate School of Management at Cornell with a Master of Business Administration Degree and I hold a BA from Colgate. As a political science major, I became very interested in a career in public service, especially in helping make government more efficient and responsive to the public. I understand that your office has been designated a reinvention lab.

Between college and graduate school I worked for 13 months as Assistant Financial Manager of a small hardware chain in upper state New York. That position required me to be a "jack-of-all-trades," at least in fiscal matters. I prepared budget projections, served as a member of a team that managed $58 million in accounts receivable and $144 million in accounts payable, and took the lead in computerizing the accounting department through installation of ACCPAC BPI accounting software.

My supervisors, colleagues, and professors have found me to be an enthusiastic, resourceful, creative team player. I would appreciate meeting with you to discuss any openings that you expect to have. Dr. Bolling said that you might also know of openings in other agencies. I will call your office next week to see if I can set up an appointment at the end of the month when I'll be in Washington, DC.

Thank you very much for considering my request. If you or your staff wish to reach me, please call (000) 000-000.

Sincerely,

Jane Anderson

Enclosure

You cannot be hired into a federal job or promoted unless you meet the requirements of the rating factors that are described on the job announcement. Let's talk about these rating or evaluation factors.

Rating Factors: Knowledge, Skills and Abilities

New hires and merit promotions are made on the basis of how applicants measure up to a set of factors, often called "Knowledge, Skills, and Abilities" (KSAs) or "Knowledge, Skills, Abilities and Other Characteristics (KSAOs)." There are two kinds of factors, but you may find them called by other names:

✎   Selective Factors are KSAs that are in addition to the minimum education and experience qualifications described in the *Qualification Standards Handbook*. You can't qualify for the position without meeting these essential factors.

✎   Quality Ranking Factors are KSAs that could be expected to increase your chances for performing well in a position, but they aren't considered essential for satisfactory performance. Applicants who have these KSAs may be ranked above those who do not, but no one may be found ineligible for not having these factors. Here's how this translates: You aren't going to get the job unless you have these factors. Competition is fierce; lots of applicants will have these factors so the pickings aren't slim.

You aren't going to get the job unless you meet the quality ranking factors.

Quality factors, which may be as few as three or four, or as many as a dozen, are the key elements in a job announcement in the federal government today. These critical job elements are the basis of an applicant's rating. Usually the selecting official (the manager who is doing the hiring) determines these factors and the weights to be assigned to each one, depending on the job to be done. See the rating guide sample.

Agencies' *Supplemental Qualifications Statements* differ widely in their practices regarding these factors. Some agencies have developed special forms for an applicant to use in describing KSAOs; other agencies accept supplements prepared by the applicant. These are called Supplemental Qualifications Statements. (*Optical Scan* questionnaires are also called Supplemental Statements, but we are not discussing these statements in this chapter.) Some agencies do not require a supplemental statement as part of the application, but you must address these factors in the Optional Form 612, the resume, or the SF-171. If the job announcement says that a supplemental qualifications statement is optional, you must write your application in such a way that the factors are clearly identified and discussed.

How Agencies Evaluate Factors

Some agencies assign specific-point-values to each factor. For example, 6 points for "outstanding" down to no points for "developmental." Other agencies assign values of "high," "medium," or "low," without regard to exact points.

Personnel specialists take into account experience, education, training and awards as they relate to the factors when they examine your application package. Often the job announcement will indicate exactly how the factors will be rated and what weights are assigned.

If you do not find this kind of specific rating information on the announcement, you may call the personnel specialist listed on the announcement and ask for the rating guide. If the agency did not provide its own supplemental qualifications statement for you to use, ask if any special items must be included. For example, some agencies require a supervisor's name and phone number to verify the experience you describe and some require an original signature and date, even though you signed the Optional Form or SF-171.

SAMPLE RATING GUIDE

Program Analyst
GS-345-13 PD# 123850
BERC, Regulations Staff, Coverage & Analysis Branch

I. RATING CRITERIA FOR EXPERIENCE AND APPRAISAL   MAXIMUM 50 POINTS

   1. Ability to prepare written products, e.g., memoranda, policies, regulations or option papers.

   2. Ability to analyze issues and develop/present recommendations or solutions. (CRITICAL)

   3. Ability to establish and maintain liaison with internal and/or external components. (CRITICAL)

CREDIT FOR EXPERIENCE		CREDIT FOR APPRAISAL	
Quality Level	Points	Quality Level	Points
Superior	5 points	Substantially Exceeded	5 points
Above Average	3 points	Exceeded	3 points
Average	2 points	Fully Met	2 points
Developmental	0 points	Partially Met	0 points

ALL CRITICAL ELEMENTS WILL BE DOUBLE WEIGHTED.

II. TRAINING AND SELF-DEVELOPMENT   MAXIMUM 5 POINTS

Bachelors degree in a related major field of study (English, Social Sciences, Economics, Statistics, Business, etc.) MAXIMUM 5 POINTS

Associate degree in a related major field of study (English, Social Sciences, Economics, Statistics, Business, etc.) MAXIMUM 3 POINTS

One (1) point for each three (3) credit college course (not used above) or government or non-government course of 16 hours or more related to the position (English, Writing, Computers, Administration, etc.)

III . AWARDS   MAXIMUM 5 POINTS

HHS Distinguished Service Award	5 points
HHS Superior Service Award	5 points
Administrator's Citation	4 points
Quality Salary Increase	4 points
Special Achievement Award for Sustained Superior Performance	3 points
Other Special Achievement Award or Suggestion Award	2 points

ALL AWARDS MUST BE DIRECTLY RELATED TO THE POSITION BEING FILLED.

Supplemental Qualifications Forms May Not Be Necessary Someday

I believe that supplemental qualifications statements are on the endangered species list. They were developed under the old application process as a standard, one-size-fits-all form. That form was too full of information for reviewers in the agencies to find exactly what they were looking for in qualifications for a specific job. So they created another way for applicants to present specific information for the announced job. If today's job applicants truly customize their applications (Optional Form 612, resume, or SF-171) with information that is relevant to the announced job, supplemental qualifications statements will not be needed. However, for now they survived the changes in the federal hiring process. The future form may be the optical scan variety.

How to Format and Write a Supplemental Qualifications Statement

If the job announcement you're working from does not provide its own supplemental qualifications statement, here are the kinds of information some agencies request:

- Your name, phone number, present job (title/series/grade), position sought and announcement number.

- Space for you to list each KSA that appeared in the job announcement and space beside or under each factor for your description. Provide your pertinent experience, training, awards, or outside activities (including dates) for each KSA.

- The name of the supervisor or other official (this could be a colleague) who can verify the information your provide. (Don't volunteer this information unless the agency asks for it.)

- Your signature and date signed. (Don't sign your statement unless the agency asks for it. In the new federal hiring process, signatures are not usually needed until you are narrowed down as a candidate. At that time you sign the *Declaration of Federal Employment*.)

If you develop your own form:

- Use one page or less for each announced factor, following the exact sequence of the factors in the job announcement. That is, start with factor one and proceed.

- Use either a vertical format (up and down like a letter) or a horizontal format (sideways on the paper).

- Number the pages.

- Organize your material under headings for each factor. Typical headings include Experience, Education, Training, Awards/Recognition, and Outside Activities.

- Write either narrative paragraphs, using the personal pronoun "I" if you are comfortable with this, or bullets starting with a verb to emphasize each point.

- Use or paraphrase words from the job announcement or position classification standards, but don't copy whole phrases without personalizing to fit your experiences.

- Use strong verbs, such as "directed," "managed," "administered," and "coordinated," and draw from the customer-focused career vocabulary of the 90s. See Chapter 7.

- Scope or summarize your qualifications in the first paragraph or bullet. For example, if the factor is "ability to motivate and supervise staff" you might begin with:

  > *I have had a total of 5 years supervisory experience—in business as director of a graphics department for ABC Advertising Agency and 2 years in my current position as art director for the Defense Mapping Agency.*

Then, in your subsequent bullets or paragraphs, tell how many people you supervised in each supervisory position, at what grade levels, and with what results for each position or activity. Describe any special qualities you have in coaching and motivating your staff as individuals and teams to satisfy customers, improve processes and services, cut costs, increase productivity, meet the goals of the agency, and so on.

If you have had little or no supervisory experience, then you must show your experience in coordinating an activity, leading a team, or serving as president of an organization. You should also show any courses or training which apply to management or supervision.

- Fill with personal examples telling how many, how much, and how often and all geared to the job you're aiming for. Follow the writing tips in Chapter 4 for completing Optional Form 612.

A Case Study: How Bill Rewrote His Supplemental Qualifications Statement

A few years ago, a person in another federal agency came to me to critique his SF-171 and a supplemental qualifications statement for a job he wanted. Actually, he was already in the position in an acting capacity, but the job was being competed, and he wanted to make sure that his application would put him in the job on a permanent basis.

The position was a GS-9 Supervisory Property Management Specialist and he didn't have any supervisory experience except for the brief period that he had been acting in the job. His SF-171 was complete, but not written in a personal way. It mainly captured the duties and responsibilities that almost anyone would have had in similar positions. He didn't have time to rewrite it, so he wanted to write an outstanding supplemental statement to highlight the five Supplemental Evaluation Factors listed on the job announcement.

The five factors were:

1. Technical knowledge of federal property management programs, practices, and principles relating to inventory and accountability, excess/surplus property disposal, property acquisition and transfers, office relocations (moves), and warehousing.
2. Skill in written communications.
3. General knowledge of ADP concepts and equipment to develop or operate automated office services systems.
4. Ability to develop and supervise a staff of professionals and support personnel.
5. Ability to maintain effective relationships with a variety of management levels, diverse backgrounds, and divergent points of view.

I read his first draft, and my critique only took a few minutes. For each factor, it was obvious that he had done a good job of thinking through his total experience and pulling out those activities and accomplishments that supported or demonstrated the required skills. The descriptions, however, were too formal and sounded too much like the content of a job description. He needed to personalize his comments, and to add numbers, dates and other facts that fit specific situations.

I suggested that he look again at what he had written and apply these questions to each statement:

- What?
- When?
- Where?
- How much?
- How often?
- What resulted?
- Do you have any examples?
- Do you have any volunteer experience or outside activities that would fit any of the factors? If so, add them.
- Do you have any training or awards that relate to the factors? If so, add them.

Several months later I asked him if he got the job and he said yes. I asked him if he would let me see what he had written on the basis of the above questions. When I saw what a good job he had done, I asked him if he would let me include these factors in *Promote Yourself!*, a book I wrote in 1988. I told him I would change his name to "Bill" and not identify his agency. I got a lot of positive feedback from this example, so I am recycling it for this book.

Here are "Bill's" first try and his revised draft for each evaluation factor. Compare these before and after samples carefully. You will find that it really makes a difference to provide details! Following Bill's before and after samples, you will find an additional sample Supplemental Qualifications Statement prepared by "Laura S. Murphy."

Bill's First Try at Factor 1

Position: Supervisory Property Management Specialist GS-1101-9
Announcement Number: 00-00 (0)

William A. Jones   SS#: 000-00-0000

1.   Technical knowledge of federal property management programs, practices, and principles relating to inventory and accountability, excess/surplus property disposal, property acquisition and transfers, office relocations (moves), and warehousing.

*   Performed two regional office closings, taking inventory, arranging for the transfer company, and coordinating the actual transfer of property to various locations throughout the country.

*   Conduct on-going inventories of current Office of the Secretary (OS) warehouse in order to maintain for the immediate Office of the Secretary a supply of those property items I determine must be available at all times for any possible move, for an incoming official.

*   Determine the possible future accountable property needs of offices under the Secretarial level keeping the property in stock or acquiring it from GSA.

*   Determine which property is not needed, excessing or disposing of it using GSA, departmental and office regulations.

Bill's Revised Factor 1

Position: Supervisory Property Management Specialist, GS-1101-9
Announcement Number: 00-00 (0)

William A. Jones   SS#: 000-00-0000

1.   Technical knowledge of Federal property management programs, practices, and
         principles relating to inventory and accountability, excess/surplus property
         disposal, property acquisition and transfers, office relocations (moves), and
         warehousing.

In present position, as Acting Supervisory Property Management Specialist (Block A):

•   Serve as custodial officer for over 40,000 pieces of accountable property valued at
        over $16 million.

•   Performed one on-site regional office closing in March 1988. Closed the Office of
        _____ in Maine, transferring over 60 property items valued at over $27,000.
        Sixty items were transferred and shipped to headquarters, and one item was
        transferred to the Birmingham, Alabama, office.

•   Performed one on-site regional office closing in June 1988. Closed the Office of
        _____ in California, transferring 99 property items valued at over $25,800. I
        transferred 40 property items to Sacramento, California; 10 to Columbia, South
        Carolina; 4 to Atlanta, Georgia; 35 to the Office of the Secretary (OS) in Portland,
        Oregon, and 20 to the General Services Administration (GSA) regional office.

•   Conduct on-going inventories of current OS warehouse in order to maintain a
        supply of the most requested property items to be prepared for any possible
        moves, the creation of task forces or the appointment of a new incoming official.

•   By reviewing Responsible Officers' (ROs) requisitions and memoranda request-
        ing surplus property, I determine the possible future accountable property needs
        of the ROs offices, keeping the property in stock or acquiring additional furniture
        from the GSA schedule.

•   Determine which property is not needed, excessing or disposing of it using GSA,
        Departmental and office regulations. So far in 1988, I have disposed to GSA over
        400 pieces of equipment that were in poor condition, obsolete or no longer
        requested.

Training

8-hour personal property seminar, Dept. of Health and Human Services, April 1988
40-hour property management course, GSA, July 1987 (certificate)
24-hour fleet management course, GSA, March 1986 (certificate)

Bill's First Try at Factor 2

2.   Skill in written communications.

- Developed and wrote nationwide policy in the form of the vehicle management chapter of the nationwide Office of the Secretary handbook.

- Wrote the internal control report on vehicle management in the Office of the Secretary.

- Compose memoranda and letters to various Departmental heads for the signatures of the Director, Division of Administrative services and the Branch Chief.

- Give written instructions with deadlines for filling furniture requests, handling office moves and arranging rooms for official ceremonies to warehouse subordinates and the moving unit.

- Write detailed field trip reports.

- Correspond by letters with contract leasing officials in ordering new vehicles for the immediate Office of the Secretary.

Bill's Revised Factor 2

2.   Skill in written communications.

In present position as Acting Supervisory Property Management Specialist (Block A):

- On a regular basis, compose memoranda and letters to various Departmental heads for my signature and for the signatures of the Director, Division of Administrative Services; Chief, Division of General Services and the Chief, Branch of Office Services.

- On an on-going basis, give written instructions and deadlines to two warehouse subordinates for filling furniture requests, three moving unit subordinates as well as the head of the contract laborers for handling office moves and arranging the auditorium and the Secretary's conference room for official ceremonies, press conferences, luncheon's or dinners.

- Correspond by letter with four major automobile contract leasing officials in ordering new vehicles for the immediate Office of the Secretary.

- Wrote one detailed trip report on the Durham, North Carolina office closing, in February 1988.

In previous position as Vehicle and Property Management Assistant (Block B):

- Developed and wrote nationwide policy in the form of the 20-page chapter on property management of the Office of Secretary 1987 Manual which was distributed nationwide as well as headquarters.

- Wrote the internal control report on vehicle management in the Office of the Secretary in 1987.

- Composed on a regular basis memoranda and letters to various Departmental heads for the signature of the Director, Division of Administrative Services.

- Corresponded by letter with four major automobile contract leasing officials in ordering new vehicles for the immediate OS.

Training

8-hour seminar, "How to Write Reports," US Department of Agriculture, June 1985.

Bill's First Try at Factor 3

3.   General knowledge of ADP concepts and equipment to develop or operate automated office services systems.

- Manage/supervise a computer-based accountable coding system that is used to simplify inventorying and tracking all accountable property nationwide in offices that report to the Office of the Secretary. Review these reports periodically.

- Review requisitions, receiving and accounts payable forms that are transmitted via the automated system, making immediate decisions when there are problems with items requested.

- Completed 4-hour computer literacy course.

Bill's Revised Factor 3

3. General knowledge of ADP concepts and equipment to develop or operate automated office services systems.

In present position as Acting Supervisory Property Management Specialist (Block A):

- Manage/supervise a computer based accountable coding system that is used to simplify counting and tracking all accountable property nationwide in offices that report to the Office of the Secretary. Review these reports periodically.

- Review requisitions, receiving and accounts payable forms that are transmitted via the automated system, making immediate decisions when there are problems with items requested.

Training

4-hour computer literacy course, U.S. Department of Agriculture, January 1988.

Bill's First Try at Factor 4

4.   Ability to develop and supervise a staff of professionals and support personnel.

- Made Acting Branch Chief, Branch of Office Services, with the responsibility for the assignment and distribution of work, administration of leave policies and development and implementation of reporting requirements and procedures, for over 16 employees in 5 sections for 1 week.

- As Acting Supervisory Property Management Specialist, I supervise 12 employees in 4 sections.

- Conduct bi-weekly staff meetings with subordinates, inviting input and ideas from everyone.

- Set up a class to train summer employees to conduct office property inventories of office property for the automated accountable property system.

- Located and required that all drivers for the Office of the Secretary take a defensive driving course.

- Recommended other classes for various employees to enhance their career development.

- As head chauffeur to the Secretary, I supervised two motor vehicle operators. My responsibilities included coordinating the ordering of vehicles with Office Services personnel, assuring vehicles were clean and mechanically ready at all times; assuring that the drivers took leave on a planned basis, arranging for driver coverage for high ranking officials when they were off or for the Secretary if I were to be off; planned routes when necessary to ensure the quickest and safest way to our destination.

Bill's Revised Factor 4

4.   Ability to develop and supervise a staff of professionals and support personnel.

In present position as Acting Supervisory Property Management Specialist (Block A):

- Served as Acting Chief, Branch of Office Services from April 4-8, 1988, with the responsibility for assigning work, administering leave policies and developing and implementing reporting requirements and procedures, for 15 employees in grades GS-2 through GS-12 in 5 sections.

- As Acting Supervisory Property Management Specialist, I supervise 12 employees in grades GS-2 through GS-9 in 4 sections. Assign and distribute work, administer leave policies and develop and implement reporting requirements and procedures.

- Conduct bi-weekly staff meetings, inviting input and ideas from everyone.

- Set-up a 3-day class to train three summer employees in May 1988 to conduct inventories of office property for the automated accountable property system. Recommended other classes, such as report writing and time management, for various employees to enhance their career development.

In previous position as Vehicle and Property Management Assistant (Block B)

- Counseled former GS-5 secretary who was having severe problems on the job.

- Located defensive driving course taught by GSA. Required that 15 drivers for the OS complete the course.

In previous position as Head Chauffeur (Blocks E, F, G): From 1977 to 1983, as head chauffeur to the Secretary, I supervised two motor vehicle operators. My responsibilities included coordinating the ordering of vehicles with Office Services personnel, assuring that vehicles were clean and mechanically ready at all times; assuring that the drivers took leave on a planned basis, arranging for driver coverage for high ranking officials when the drivers were off or for the Secretary if I had to be off; planned routes when necessary to ensure the quickest and safest way to our destination.

Training

Certificates: 24-hour managerial problem solving course, Health and Human Services, Jan. 1988; 24-hour time management course, Health and Human Services, Feb. 1988.

Bill's First Try at Factor 5

5.   Ability to maintain effective relationships with a variety of management levels, diverse backgrounds, and divergent points of view.

●   Speak directly with the Secretary and the Under Secretary about ordering of their officially assigned vehicles.

●   Meet with the Assistant Secretaries' administrative assistants in order to organize press conferences, official luncheons and to fill certain property requests.

●   Talk with GSA property officials to request authority to scrap or excess property.

●   Negotiate with the major automobile contract leasers prior to formal written communications to locate the most economical leasing program.

●   Contact vendors for various office furnishings, i.e., carpet installation, systems furniture installation.

●   Have driven and maintained close working relationships with two former Secretaries, two former under Secretaries and a former White House National Security advisor, as well as their official guests at all levels of federal, state and local government.

Bill's Revised Factor 5

5.   Ability to maintain effective relationships with a variety of management levels, diverse backgrounds, and divergent points of view.

In present position as Acting Supervisory Property Management Specialist (Block A) and in previous position as Vehicle and Property Management Specialist (Block B):

- From time-to-time speak directly with the Secretary and the Under Secretary about the ordering of their officially assigned vehicles. Also meet with the Assistant Secretaries' administrative assistants in order to organize press conferences, official luncheons and to fill certain property requests.

- Talk with GSA property officials to request authority to scrap or excess property.

- Negotiate with four major automobile contract leasers prior to formal written communications to locate the most economical leasing program.

- Contact various vendors for office furnishings, i.e., carpet purchasing, carpet installation, systems furniture installation; and vehicle vendors for performing the required vehicle maintenance.

In previous positions as Head Chauffeur and Chauffeur from 19__ to ___ (Blocks E, F, G, and H), I drove and maintained close working relationships with two Secretaries, two Under Secretaries and the President's National Security Advisor, as well as their official guests from all levels of national, state and local government.

Volunteer Activities

- From Sept. 1985 to the present, I have been a volunteer with the Department of _____ Federal Credit Union, serving on the credit committee with responsibilities for approving or disapproving loans.

- From November 1986 to 1988, I was on the Architectural and Environmental Control Committee of the Laurel Condo Association. My responsibilities include approving/disapproving requests for property additions, i.e., decks, porches, doors, yard structures, using guidelines established by the association. Maintained an effective relationship with the condo board and 200 Association members.

Awards

- Received 10 letters of appreciation, Dept. of _____, 1985-87.
- Received Special Achievement Awards, Dept. of _____, 1975, 1977-80.
- Received outstanding performance ratings, 1976 through 1985.

Sample Supplemental Qualifications Statement

Laura S. Murphy, SSN 000-00-0000

Department of Parks and Recreation, Announcement No.: DPR 88-25
Accounting Officer GM-14

Factor 1: Knowledge of fundamental and diversified professional financial management concepts, theories and practices to achieve planning, forecasting and other management objectives.

Specific Accomplishments:

Many of my previous positions have demonstrated a knowledge of fundamental and diversified professional financial management concepts, theories and practices. In my current position of Budget Officer and Chief of the Budget and Data Analysis Branch of the U.S. Department of Parks and Recreation, I hold responsibility for constantly changing budgets which are dependent upon program levels and budgets of other agencies. Plan, present, justify and execute the agency budget, fiscal support activities, and development and administration of automated data processing activities, and promote sound fiscal management through assured compliance with established standards.

As Budget Officer for Capitol Hospital, I provided hospital management with a monthly financial plan and supervised administration of that plan. After gathering necessary material, developed financial predictions and established needs of the hospital and forwarded this information and my recommendations to administrators and the Superintendent of the Hospital.

While Accounting Officer for Capitol Hospital, I assisted in most of the previously mentioned activities in preparation for promotion to the Budget Officer position.

Education and Training:

U.S. Parks and Recreation Graduate School
    See Attachment A - Item 31
    Advanced Certificate of Accomplishment in Accounting

Passed 510 Accounting test in May 1972

Passed CPA Exam in November 1987 - Certification pending

Laura S. Murphy, 000-00-0000

Factor 2: Knowledge of federal budget process in order to direct the formulation, justification, presentation, and execution of an agency-level budget.

Specific Accomplishments:

The past nine years have demonstrated my knowledge of the federal budget process and necessary activities for an agency-level budget. In my current position as Budget Officer and Chief of the Budget and Data Analysis Branch of the U.S. Department of Parks and Recreation, I manage daily requirements of the agency's budget administration, including interaction with supporting agencies and account representatives. I also prepare and present the budget for approval by the Administrator, OMB, and Congress. Determine impact of current legislation on the proposed or approved budget.

While Budget Officer for Capitol Hospital, I performed many of the duties involved in my present position. Managed a budget of over $136M for salaries and expenses and over $66M for building and construction. Performed necessary activities to have these budgets approved and supported their administration through proper and necessary documentation as mandated by the federal agencies involved.

Education and Training:

U.S. Parks and Recreation Graduate School
     Budgetary Procedures, Formulation and Presentation - 1980
     Congress and the Budget - 1980

Office of Personal Management -
     Seminar on Federal Appropriation Law - 1985

Congressional Quarterly Course -
     The Congressional Budget Process Seminar - 1981

Laura S. Murphy, 000-00-0000

Factor 3: Ability to deal effectively with high-level budget contacts within the Department, outside the Department, i.e., the U.S. Treasury, Office of Financial Management, and with international organizations.

Specific Accomplishments:

All of my previous positions have offered an opportunity to deal with officials in the upper levels of budgetary preparation. My current position brings me into direct contact with Department officials, Treasury Department officials, members of Congress, and members of other agencies who have interest in the administration of Parks and Recreation's budget. Often, disagreements concerning the administration or approval of the budget requests must be diffused, and I am the agency representative in matters concerning the budget; therefore, I must deal diplomatically and effectively with these persons in order to come to a mutually agreeable situation.

In my positions at Capitol Hospital, I was directly involved in Congressional briefings and advising of Division Directors and Hospital Administrators as the Budget Officer for the hospital. This position also required effective communication and interaction with these officials. While Assistant Finance Officer, I assisted in the pursuance of these duties and developed the required techniques for this interaction.

Factor 4: Skill in directing automated accounting system of a complex organization.

Specific Accomplishments:

The best example of my skill in directing automated accounting systems of a complex organization is my position as Budget Officer at Capitol Hospital, where I not only directed the use of the system, but assisted in its implementation. I evaluated its daily and monthly performance and efficiency in the administration of the complex budget of the National Institute of Health which was in a constant state of change in response to factors in other departments and demands by Health Organizations and the courts.

In my position as Budget Officer for Capitol Hospital, I also prepared reports and forecasts with the assistance of an IBM-PC.

Education and Training:

Office of Personnel Management
    Computer Course for Budget Officers and Staff - 1984
    Introduction to Automatic Data Processing (ADP) - 1978
    Automated Accounting Systems - 1978

Chapter Six
Resumes For Uncle Sam
— Yes, No, and Maybe

Until 1995, the federal government did not accept resumes for a job application. Now you can choose whatever application you wish: a resume, the new Optional Form, or if you have software or paper copies of the abandoned Standard Form 171, you can use that.

So far, so good. There is one problem with using a resume, however. The formula for a federal-style resume bears no resemblance to the short, snappy resume used in the private sector. Industrial-strength resumes are short, but powerful. In one or two pages you present results-oriented highlights of your career focused on a specific job or career field. Experts tell us that you have only 30 to 60 seconds to keep your prospective employer's attention. In the private sector, resumes are "looked at," not usually read carefully, according to Kathryn K. Troutman, President of The Resume Place, Inc. in Washington, DC. The main goal of a resume is to attract enough attention to get you an interview. Details—such as addresses of previous employers and your social security number, as examples—can be provided later.

The new federal resume is not planned to be just an attention getter. It is a full-fledged application requiring numerous details. It is basically a form without a format. If you fail to provide all the information requested in the job announcement or listed in the new flyer, *Applying for a Federal Job*, the agency may reject your application. The information you must present in the resume is the same as that required in the new Optional Form 612. The exception is that you do not have to certify by signature on a resume that the information you have provided is correct. This certification is actually not needed at the beginning of the process. Before an agency appoints you to a federal job, you will have to answer other questions and sign the *Declaration for Federal Employment*.

Three Application Options

If the job you want requires a paper application, a resume is one of three options. You must decide which is best for you:

A federal-style resume bears no resemblance to the short, snappy resume used in the private sector.

Option 1: Yes, Write a Resume

Write a resume targeted to the requirements of the job announcement. Here you can be as creative as you wish in formatting, assuming you use common sense. Use a simple design, white space, highlighting techniques like bolding for emphasis, and restraint when it comes to fancy fonts and gimmicky graphics. The *Quick and Easy Federal Job Application Kit* also includes help for federal resumes or you can find other resume software to make your job easier. Just be careful not to leave out any required information. Also, there are many excellent books and software packages on resume preparation. Many resume services are not tuned in yet to the new federal format. Don't use the service unless it is. One such service is The Resume Place, Inc., in Washington, DC. It has followed the new federal hiring procedures very closely and can offer assistance with the Optional Form or the new federal-style resume.

I also highly recommend that you use a combined chronological-functional resume format using an abbreviated version of the announced special rating factors (qualifications) as functional headings. See below for more information about this format.

Option 2: No, Use the Optional Form

Complete the Optional Form 612 targeted to the requirements of the job announcement. You have a basic structure to work with and it's standardized so that reviewers can find everything. I recommend a software package, the *Quick and Easy Federal Job Application Kit,* to provide tips and expand the blocks as necessary to get information in without using cumbersome attachment sheets.

Option 3: Use Both

Complete the Optional Form 612 and top it with a snappy, private sector-style, one-page resume focusing on key points. This will not get you a single extra point in the review process, but it has many advantages. The initial reviewer will probably ignore it, but the manager who will make the final selection from the list of most qualified applicants, will love not having to plow through several pages of details. Another good use of a short, snappy cover letter and a one or two-page resume has nothing to do with an announced job. You could use the letter and resume to get in touch with federal managers to interview them about what they do and to ask their advice about pursuing a federal career in their line of work. You get names by talking to people at conferences, getting people you know to refer you, doing agency research in publications like the *U.S. Government Manual,* and calling the agency's public information office. See Chapter 8 for details.

Regular rules don't apply to federal

In considering these options, you have one important thing to ponder: If you use a resume, should you follow the same sequence as that of Optional Form 612 or should you develop your own format? The advantage in following the sequence of the form is that reviewers don't have to struggle to make sure you haven't left anything out and can evaluate your qualifications fairly, quickly, and easily. The disadvantage is that you are using valuable, up-front space for details that don't go on private sector resumes—like your Social Security number, for example.

Which Option is Best for You?

Based on this important consideration I would use the third option suggested above for most federal job applications—the Optional Form topped with a dynamite one-page resume featuring career highlights that relate to the targeted job. However, this is only a suggestion. Resumes are brand new in the federal hiring process. The jury isn't in on what works best.

As we've just seen, regular rules don't apply to federal resumes. However, it's important to review conventional resume wisdom, including the different types of resumes used in the business world. If you are a federal employee, this information will also be helpful if you plan to convert your Standard Form 171 to a resume format to apply for promotions or job changes. It will also help if you are retiring or facing a reduction-in-force (RIF). You will need a resume to help search for a job in the private sector. If you have developed and maintained a good Standard Form 171 during your federal career, it will serve as a good start in building an equally-effective resume. Here's a tip from resume pro Kathryn Troutman, President of the Resume Place, Inc., in Washington, DC: Have a colleague critique the resume you write. "Sometimes it's difficult to be objective about your own background," she says. "Someone else who is seeing it for the first time may be able to offer advice about what does or doesn't jump off the page."

Actually, regular rules don't always apply to private sector resumes anymore, what with the advent of software that can scan and file resumes electronically. But that's another story, and if you want to know more, read Joyce Lain Kennedy and Thomas J. Morrow's 1994 book, *Electronic Resume Revolution*, published by John Wiley & Sons, Inc., New York. The federal counterpart to this electronic screening wizardry is optical scanning of forms, not resumes. See Chapter 3.

Traditional Private Sector Resume Formats

Private sector resumes usually come in three basic formats:

Chronological. A chronological format starts with the most recent experience and goes back in reverse chronological order. Each job is described as you go. This is a straight forward approach if you have a strong background in your field—the right job titles, the right agencies or companies, the right number of years in each job, and no breaks in employment. If you have a work background that has followed an orderly progression and your new job goals are very much in line with your background, then a chronological resume might be a good choice for you.

Functional. This format pulls skills, accomplishments, and responsibilities out of the reverse chronological date format and describes the overall experience under functional areas of experience that relate to the job objective. This approach is excellent if you are unemployed or have several distinct areas of expertise. The functional resume focuses on your skills and areas of expertise, without emphasizing the sequence of your experience (although you could include work sites and organizations in your functional writeups and put dates in parentheses). This format closely resembles the formats used to describe knowledge, skills and abilities (KSAs) in supplemental qualifications statements.

This format is useful in the private sector for those who want to change fields, return to a previous career, emphasize previous experience, hide short-term dates or temporary, unimportant jobs, or play down anything (agency name, titles, jobs, dates). However, the federal resume *requires* you to include these details if this experience is related to the job you are targeting.

Combined Chronological-Functional. This format combines features from each of the other two types of resumes. You give a work history, with dates in reverse chronological order, but you do not describe your accomplishments under each job. The history can appear near the beginning or the end of the resume, depending on what you want to emphasize. Describe your achievements in several functional blocks drawn from various times in your career. This is a versatile format and useful in a variety of situations.

Sample Outlines for Federal Resumes

On the next pages you will find sample chronological and combined chronological-functional resume outlines that would be suitable for applying for a federal job.

Sample Federal Chronological Resume Outline
Name and Personal Data

Put your name, address, and work and home phones.

Objective

Many private sector resumes currently omit an objective, but in a federal resume your objective is the title and announcement number of the job you have targeted. If this is an exploratory resume (no announced job), omit an objective and add a very short skills summary.

Experience

Put your paid and nonpaid work history in reverse chronological order, with title (series and grade if federal employee), name of organization, city and state, supervisor's name and phone number, and dates worked for each position. Include only those jobs that relate to the targeted job, concentrating on the most recent if possible. Add a few bullets under each job emphasizing accomplishments, results, and skills as expressed in the special rating factors and other required qualifications. Mention job-related awards.

Education and Training

List degrees, schools, and training (including addresses and dates), emphasizing those that relate to the targeted job. Mention any scholastic honors or memberships in scholarly organizations.

School, Professional, Technical, and Community Organizations and Affiliations

List memberships and leadership roles and activities.

Other Information

Under one or more headings as needed, provide social security number, citizenship, veterans' preference, supervisors' names (if not supplied under experience), publications, speaking experience, hobbies, and other information you couldn't find a place for above if it is required or related to the targeted job.

Sample Federal Chronological-Functional Resume Outline

Name and Personal Data

Put your name, address, and work and home phones.

Objective

Many private sector resumes currently omit an objective, but in a federal resume your objective is the title and announcement number of the job you have targeted. If this is an exploratory resume (no announced job), omit an objective and add a very short skills summary.

Areas of Skills and Experience

As sub-headings, select three or four functional titles or skills areas such as "Training," "Benefits Administration," and "Personnel," based on the required rating factors from the job announcement. It may be possible to make functional headings from the factors. For example, the rating factor *Knowledge of Federal budget process in order to direct the formulation, justification, presentation, and execution of an agency-level budget* and the rating factor *Ability to deal effectively with high-level budget contacts within the Department, outside the Department, i.e., the U.S. Treasury, Office of Financial Management, and with international organizations* could become one functional heading, **Federal Budget Process**.

Draw from your paid and nonpaid work history and your school and community activities to write a few bullets under each functional area, emphasizing accomplishments, results, and skills as expressed in the special rating factors and other required qualifications. Mention job-related awards, courses, and training that relate to each area, but do not duplicate items under "Education and Training" below. Choose the most appropriate place to highlight these items.

Experience History (or Employment History)

List without commentary your paid and nonpaid work history in reverse chronological order, with title (series and grade if federal employee), name of organization, city and state (I'm hoping you can get away without a full address), and dates worked for each position. Include only those jobs that relate to the targeted job, concentrating on the most recent if possible. Add supervisors' names and phone numbers as part of the list.

Education and Training

List degrees, schools, and training (including addresses and dates), emphasizing those that relate to the targeted job. Mention any scholastic honors or memberships in scholarly organizations. Put **Education and Training** right after **Objective** if your education is your major qualifying factor.

Other Information

Under one or more headings as needed, provide social security number, citizenship, veterans preference, supervisors' names and phone numbers (if not supplied under experience), publications, speaking experience, hobbies, and other information you couldn't find a place for above if it is required or related to the targeted job.

Resume Summary

In general, Optional Form 612 provides a suitable structure and headings for a federal resume, although less eye-catching information like your social security number should not be featured at the top of a resume. See the example that follows.

The following sample resume shows the necessary experience and skills for an entry level GS 5/7 writer-editor job. Excerpts from a job announcement come first, followed by the resume. This sample is for demonstration only. The federal agency is fictitious and I made up the attributes in the resume.

Sample Job Announcement

Opening Date: April 3, 1995
Closing Date: May 15, 1995
National Research Agency

Announcement Number: NRA-95-042
Position Title: Writer-Editor, GS-1092-5
Location: NRA, Office of the Director, Office of Publications and Public Affairs
Area of Consideration: commuting area

Duties and Responsibilities: Performs a variety of duties associated with writing, editing, producing, and distributing documents for internal and external distribution. Writes and produces camera-ready copy for news releases, fact sheets, brochures, newsletters and other publications. Researches and writes articles for internal newsletter and external magazine. Works with other writers, editors, editorial assistants, program specialists, researchers, and graphic specialists to produce audio-visuals, annual reports, strategic plans, training materials, statistical summaries, magazines, and other publications. Works with outside contractors to arrange mailings of publications and news releases. Assists in mailing or faxing information in response to media and public requests. Assembles and proofreads entries for agency directories and catalogs. Performs online literature searches.

Minimum Qualifications: Applicants must have one year of specialized experience equivalent to the next lower grade in the federal government. Specialized experience is experience that has equipped the applicant with the particular knowledge, skills, and abilities to perform successfully the duties of the position and that is related to the work of the position to be filled. The applicant must be a U.S. citizen.

Education Substitution: Successful completion of a full 4-year course of study leading to a bachelor's degree, with a major in journalism or English.

Evaluation Method: Applicants will be evaluated on knowledge, skills and abilities (KSAs) related to the position being advertised. Applicants should address the following KSAs on a separate sheet of paper and attach to Optional Form 612, Standard Form 171 or resume.

1. Ability to communicate orally and in writing.
2. Ability to plan and produce publications and other materials.
3. Skill in writing and editing.
4. Ability to use word processing or publishing software to prepare camera-ready documents and to maintain databases for distribution lists.

Louise M. Eagen

8384 Mason Court, Apt. 12, Timonium, MD 00000
(000) 000-0000 (day), (000) 000-0000 (evenings)

Objective

Writer-Editor, GS-1087-5, NRA-95-042

Skills Summary

Experienced in WordPerfect 6.0 for Windows, Harvard Graphics, PowerPoint, and DBase IV. Use Internet and CD-ROM for literature searches. Will receive BA in English, May 1995. Worked weekends and summers as proofreader/publications assistant for small publishing company. Served as reporter and art editor for college newspaper.

Experience

6/1/92-present

Proofreader and Publications Assistant, Meadows Press, 8506 York Rd., Timonium, MD, 00000. You may contact my supervisor: Edgar W. Sommers, (000) 000-0000—Work full time from June 1 until Labor Day each summer and 10 hours each week during school year for $10 an hour. Proofread or copy/edit brochures, booklets, flyers, and books.

9/6/93-present

Art Editor and Reporter (nonpaid volunteer work, 10 hours monthly), *Templeton Tower*, Templeton College, Towson, MD 00000. Faculty advisor: Agnes M. Krimm, (000) 000-0000-—Write articles and design monthly newsletter that goes to student body and local merchants. Helped circulation manager in establishing and maintaining mailing list on DBase IV.

9/1/91-5/30/92

Student Assistant, English Department, Templeton College. Supervisor: Margaret Atkins, PhD, Department Chair, (000) 000-0000—Assisted Departmental faculty with record keeping, filing, photocopying, faxing, word processing, and research as participant in student work program. Earned partial tuition waiver and minimum wage stipend for 12-15 hours a week.

Education

BA expected May 1995, Templeton College, Towson, MD 00000. Major: English; Minor: Psychology. Dean's List for four semesters.

Personal

U.S. Citizen, born in Columbia, Maryland. SSN# 000-00-000

Louise M. Eagen, page 2   SSN: 000-00-0000
Knowledge, Skills, and Abilities

1. Ability to communicate orally and in writing

As a reporter for the college newspaper, I interview students, professors, visiting lecturers, and others to write timely, interesting articles and news stories. As art editor, I am a cooperative but persuasive member of the student team that makes business and editorial decisions.

2. Ability to plan and produce publications and other materials.

As art editor and member of the newsletter team, I participate in planning and producing the newsletter. I contribute useful, creative ideas for stories, themes, layouts and work with the team to produce and distribute the newsletter monthly. As a full-time publications assistant for Meadows Press in the summer of 1994, I helped plan, produce, and distribute the winter catalog and news releases to the news media, publishing community and the company's national distributor.

3. Skill in writing and editing.

My college newspaper story on our ethnically-diverse faculty and student body was picked up by a local newspaper and its theme was the subject of an editorial. My story on campus ballroom dancing was reprinted in *Dancing, USA*. I have also received high marks from my professors for the research and writing skills that I display in the papers I write for classroom assignments. For example, my psychology professor said that a paper I wrote on anaesthesia was the best he had ever received from a freshman. As a proofreader, I use the University of Chicago Style Manual. My supervisor and the editors at Meadows Press, a small, local publishing company, have commended me for the clarity of my editorial suggestions, which go far beyond my proofreading responsibilities.

4. Ability to use word processing or publishing software to prepare camera-ready documents and to use and maintain databases for distribution lists.

I am competent and experienced in the following software and online technology based on my course work and paid and nonpaid work experience in publications:
- WordPerfect 5.2 for DOS and 6.0 for Windows, including styles, advanced macros, footnoting and indexing.
- Harvard Graphics
- Dbase IV
- CD-ROM and Internet

Chapter Seven
Visible and Invisible
Buzz Words

In this chapter, we'll discuss the kinds of words you'll use to describe your qualifications for the job you want. Some words are more powerful and appropriate than others, and if they are the "right" words, we often call them "buzz" words. These words represent concepts, actions, knowledge, and activities that agency reviewers and panelists look for to determine if you are qualified for the announced position. Some words are very obvious because many of them appear on the job announcement and the position description. I call these the "visible" buzz words and I've listed these words since I wrote my first book on federal applications, *The 171 Workbook*, in 1978.

Some words are more powerful and appropriate than others.

But in recent years, because big government is being reduced, reinvented, and reformed by citizen demand, new buzz words are emerging—words that may not yet be fully reflected in job descriptions and job announcements, and certainly not in the traditional classification standards. Yet these are powerful words, words that have a special meaning to the executives and managers who are doing the hiring. These are the citizen or customer-driven words of the 90s, and I call them the "invisible" buzz words because they may not be on the job announcements. When you use these words in your resumes, application forms, and cover letters, you show your understanding and commitment to reforms that are underway to change the way government operates and even what it does. Let's look at both the visible and invisible buzz words.

Buzz Words You Can See

As you read an agency job announcement, pay special attention to the verbs and nouns under the described duties and the quality ranking factors. Use these words to describe your experience on Optional Form 612, resumes, cover letters, and supplemental qualifications statements. Agency reviewers and panelists look for these traditional "buzz words" to determine if you are qualified for the announced position.

Parroting words, however, is not enough to demonstrate your qualifications, even if these same words are in your current job description. You need to give personal examples showing what you accomplished related to the words in the job announcement.

For example, if an announced job requires "skill in research and analysis," it isn't sufficient for you to write "skilled in research and analysis." Be specific. Give job-related examples of how you gained these skills. Here are two examples, using verbs (which are stronger words than nouns):

Researched and analyzed child abuse and neglect reporting laws in 12 states and wrote comprehensive report for County League of Women Voters. Two key recommendations were later passed by the South Carolina General Assembly and signed into law by the Governor.

As a student assistant, I researched and analyzed student data for the head of the Psychology Department. I prepared statistical analyses for school studies, devised new methods for examining data, and compiled reports that were used by the college to report to federal funding sources.

Verbs

Verbs are the most powerful words you can use in describing your qualifications. At the end of this chapter you'll find a list of compelling verbs to jog your memory about your experiences and help you move from nouns to verbs.

If you are interested in supervisory or managerial positions, some key buzz words are administer, advise, analyze, coach, communicate, coordinate, decide, develop, direct, establish, facilitate, evaluate, implement, initiate, lead, manage, motivate, negotiate, organize, oversee, persuade, plan, recommend, and supervise. These verbs are so strong they can also be used effectively to describe qualifications for almost any position at any grade level.

Donna Moore, in her book, *Take Charge of Your Own Career* (1994, Psychological Assessment Resources, Inc. Odessa, FL 33556), says that the Department of Labor divides skills into those related to (1) people, (2) data, and (3) things. Ms. Moore offers an excellent exercise with verbs, "Focus on Transferrable Skills," on page 206 of her book. It groups verbs according to skills related to people, skills related to data and skills related to things. She asks her readers to check any skills they have used in past jobs as a way of assessing their transferrable skills.

Nouns Help Too

Naturally, you should use the general and specific nouns associated with your field, such as contract specifications, budget, staffing plan, market value, business plan, filing system, rehabilitation, social services, FORTRAN, Lotus 1-2-3, instructional system, information management, property management, or law enforcement. Just be careful to avoid obtuse jargon and bureaucratic gobbledegook. Write so that anyone can read and understand what you mean.

Parroting words is not enough to demonstrate your qualifications.

Reduce, Reinvent, Reform and Other Invisible Buzz Words for the 90s

In the last decade the federal government has made real strides in adopting a more global, business-like, customer-focused view of its operations, thanks in part to the worldwide information explosion and the new, less hierarchical managerial approaches. Vice President Gore's National Performance Review recommendations and Presidential executive orders reflect this trend, as do the Government Performance and Results Act of 1993 and the Republican-controlled Congress in 1995. The current initiative to reform government activities does not appear to be a passing fancy. Support for reform is coming from both political parties, business, labor unions, and the public. No serious federal manager, worker, or job seeker can ignore the reforms that are underway to reduce government and change the way it operates. New buzz words are emerging—some too new to be reflected in the more traditional language of agency job announcements and position descriptions. Citizens are government's customers, and these new buzz words are based on customer demand for better service from a smaller, more efficient government.

These words include customer satisfaction, customer service standards, delayering, empowerment, labor-management partnerships, teamwork, flattening hierarchies, quality management, reinventing government, reinvention labs, reengineering, streamlining, benchmarking and many more. Some federal employees are already working in new ways. While these new words may not necessarily be the words that personnel specialists and application raters are looking for, they are words that managers who make the hiring decisions are interested in. The traditional, visible buzz words may help you get on a list of qualified applicants. The emerging federal career vocabulary will get the attention of the person who hires you. By all means, use these new words liberally in the *Optional Form 612*, resumes, supplemental qualifications statements, and cover letters.

These are also dynamite words to use in cover letters and resumes to get the attention of federal managers even before jobs are announced. Managers tend to save savvy letters like these for future hiring consideration.

New Role for Managers

If you are an executive or manager, or aspiring to be one, you are expected to lead, not just manage. Here are the some of the new skills expected of you:

- Focus on internal and external customers
- Help agency develop a vision
- Reengineer work as it flows horizontally through the agency, not vertically in your organizational stove pipe
- Be ready to relinquish your turf
- Coach, mentor employees
- Make information available to everyone
- Make systemic changes that improve work environment
- Develop partnerships with other groups, organizations, suppliers
- Encourage employee and agency cooperation and teamwork, not competition
- Encourage and profit from workforce diversity
- Throw away rule books
- Encourage entrepreneurial behavior and risk taking among your employees
- Let employees have responsibility
- Facilitate change
- Strive for excellence, but manage for results
- Tolerate mistakes in others
- Admit your own mistakes
- Reward learning and results
- Celebrate success

New Role for Employees

Federal employees of the 90s are expected to be leaders and innovators, not just cogs in a wheel. Here are some of the new skills and attitudes expected of federal workers:

- Focus on internal and external customers
- Participate in teams; share work and information
- Be non-judgmental and open to ideas

- Take responsibility; be trustworthy with new freedoms and empowerment
- Cooperate, don't compete
- Commit to organizational vision and mission
- Communicate with everyone in every direction
- Trust others
- Respect diversity among your fellow employees
- Pursue excellence and quality
- Go above and beyond your job description
- Accept challenges; don't be afraid to take risks
- Develop partnerships with other groups, organizations, suppliers
- Understand the big picture, not just the tasks that make up your job
- Be entrepreneurial
- Keep looking at the *way* you work and try to improve it
- Work with others to improve work processes
- Try new things; throw out what doesn't work
- Keep learning new skills and new approaches
- Be flexible about work, schedules, and work locations

Following the list of verbs, you'll find a list of the new buzz words for the 90s. Use both the visible and invisible buzz words in describing your responsibilities, duties, accomplishments, and skills.

Verbs: the Power Words

Accelerated
accepted
accompanied
accomplished
achieved
acquired
acted
adapted
added
addressed
adjudicated
adjusted
administered
advanced
advised
affected
aired
allocated
allotted
allowed
analyzed
answered
anticipated
appeared
applied
appointed
appraised
approved
arbitrated
arranged
asked
assembled
assessed
assigned
assisted
assumed
assured
attained
attracted
audited
augmented
authorized

avoided
awarded

Based
bought
briefed
broadcast
brought
budgeted
built

Called
canceled
canvassed
cataloged
caused
celebrated
centralized
certified
chaired
championed
changed
checked
chose
clarified
classified
closed
coached
codified
collaborated
collected
combined
commemorated
commended
communicated
compared
competed
compiled
completed
composed
computed
conceived
conceptualized

concluded
conducted
confirmed
considered
constructed
consulted
contacted
contained
continued
contracted
contributed
controlled
convened
converted
conveyed
convinced
cooperated
coordinated
corrected
correlated
corresponded
corroborated
counseled
counted
crafted
created
credited
critique
crosscut
crusaded
curbed
customized
cut

Dealt
debited
debugged
decentralized
decided
declared
decorated
dedicated

deduced
deemed
defeated
defended
defined
delegated
delivered
delved
demanded
demonstrated
described
designated
designed
determined
developed
devised
diagnosed
directed
discovered
discussed
disseminated
distributed
divided
documented
doubled
drafted
drove
drew

Earned
edited
educated
effected
elevated
eliminated
emerged
employed
empowered
enabled
enacted
encompassed
encouraged

endeavored
endorsed
enforced
engaged
engineered
enlarged
enlisted
enlivened
ensured
entered
equipped
established
estimated
evaluated
examined
exceeded
excelled
executed
exhibited
expanded
expedited
experienced
experimented
explained
explored
expressed
extended
extracted

Faced

facilitated
fashioned
featured
filed
filled
filmed
financed
finished
fitted
focused
forced
forecast
forged
formulated
fostered

fought
found
founded
fulfilled
furnished
furthered

Garnered

gathered
generated
ghostwrote
governed
graded
graduated
granted
guaranteed
guarded
guided

Handled

headed
helped
hired
hosted

Identified

illustrated
implemented
improved
improvised
incorporated
increased
indexed
indicated
influenced
informed
initiated
insisted
inspected
inspired
installed
instructed
insured

integrated
intensified
interacted
interpreted
interviewed
introduced
invented
inventoried
invested
investigated
involved
issued

Joined

justified

Kept

Launched

learned
leased
lectured
led
let
levied
licensed
linked
listed
located
logged

Made

maintained
managed
mandated
manufactured
marketed
mastered
matched
measured
mediated
mentioned
mentored

met
modeled
modified
molded
monitored
motivated
moved

Named

negotiated

Observed

obtained
offered
officiated
opened
operated
ordered
organized
outlined
overcame
oversaw

Paid

participated
passed
perceived
perfected
performed
persuaded
phased in/out
piloted
pioneered
placed
planned
polled
portrayed
practiced
prepared
presented
presided
prevented
priced

printed
processed
procured
produced
programmed
prohibited
projected
promoted
prompted
proposed
prosecuted
protected
provided
publicized
published
purchased
put

Qualified

Ranked
rated
recast
received
recognized
recommended
reconciled
recorded
recruited
reduced
referred

regulated
related
released
removed
renegotiated
reorganized
repaired
replaced
replied
reported
represented
requested
required
researched
resolved
responded
restricted
revamped
reversed
reviewed
revised

Salvaged
saved
scheduled
screened
sealed
secured
selected
served
serviced
set

settled
set up
signed
simplified
sold
solved
sorted
sought
specified
spoke
staffed
started
stimulated
strengthened
strictured
studied
submitted
substituted
succeeded
suggested
summarized
supervised
surpassed
surveyed
synthesized

Tackled
targeted
taught
tested
theorized
toured

traced
trained
transcribed
transferred
translated
transported
trapped
traveled
treated
tried
triggered
tripled
turned
typed

Unified

updated
upgraded
used

Verified
visited
volunteered

Went
won
worked
wrote

Customer-Centered Buzz Words

Accelerate

acceleration
align
alignment
assess
assessment

Baldrige criteria

benchmark
benchmarking
best practices
bottom-up
bulletin board
business plan
business processes
business process
    improvement

Change

change agent
change process
chaos
collaborate
collaboration
communicate (up, down,
    sideways)
communication
competition
competitive
consensus
cooperate
cooperation
continuous improvement
core competencies
core processes
cost effective
create
creativity
cross agency
cross sector
culture

culture change
culture shift
customer
customer-centered
customer-driven
customer-focused
customer satisfaction
customer service
customer service
    standards
customer survey
cutting red tape

Data

data-driven
decentralize
delayer
delegate
delegation
devolution
distance learning
diversity
downsizing

Effective

effectiveness
efficiency
efficient
electronic bulletin boards
electronic networks
eliminate
employee empowerment
employee involvement
employee responsibility
empower
empowerment
entrepreneurial
    government
excel
excellence
external customers

Fact-based

facts
fast service
feedback
fee-for-service
flattening hierarchies
flattening organizational
    stovepipes
flattening organizations
flexibility
focus groups
frontline
frontline employees

Generalist

global
goals
government that works
    better and costs less

High-performing
    organization
holistic
Hoshin planning

Improve

improvement
incremental
    improvements
information
Information Age
information highway
initiate
initiative
innovate
innovation
integrate (programs, ideas)
integration
interagency
intergovernmental
internal customers

internal markets
international
Internet

Knowledge
Knowledge Age

Labor-management
    cooperation
labor-management
    partnerships
leadership (at all levels)
learning
learning organization
less government
lifetime learning

Malcolm Baldrige Na-
    tional Quality Award
managing for results
measure
measuring outcomes
measurement
mission
multi-skilled (work force)

National Performance
    Review
network
networking

Online
organizational change
organizational culture
outcomes
out-of-the-box thinking

Partnerships
people

perform
performance
Presidential Award for
    Quality
President's Quality Award
program
priority
private sector partners
privatize
process
process improvement
productive
productivity
public demand
purpose

Quality
Quality Improvement
    Prototype Award
quality leadership
quality management
quality principles
quality tools

Rapid response
reduce
reengineer
reengineering
reinvent
reinventing government
reinvention
reinvention labs
reform
renewal
reorder priorities
responsibility
results
results-oriented
rightsizing
risk

risk-taking

Satellite broadcast
self-managed teams
self-motivated
statistical process control
statistics
strategic planning
strategic vision
strategy
streamline
streamlining
system
systemic
systems change
systems thinking

Team
teamwork
technological change
technology
telecommunication
total quality
Total Quality
    Management
Total Quality Leadership
transform
transformation
trust

Values
virtual government
vision
visioning

Whitewater
workforce diversity
world
worldwide

Chapter Eight
Steps to Success:
How To Find a Federal Job

Getting a job in the federal government is like getting a job in the private sector. Hiring decisions are made by people, not by pieces of paper or computers. Managers don't hire anyone they haven't met, either before the job was announced or in a formal job interview. You need to talk with people to get good leads; you need to interview people to get information. In other words, you need to make contacts.

You need to make contacts.

This may seem strange in a civil service system based on merit, but actually the system is quite pliable. There are a lot more qualified people than there are jobs. Thus, another kind of competition kicks in. You are competing with eager, well-qualified candidates, many of whom have targeted the job you want. Successful job hunters make personal contacts with federal personnel officials who know the hiring system and federal managers who plan what workers they need and make the hiring decisions. Like successful job hunters in the private sector, they often start making contacts before jobs are announced. They tell everyone they know—relatives, friends, colleagues, acquaintances—that they are looking for a job. They also ask for advice from people in their career fields or others who can guide them.

In this chapter we'll look at the major steps to finding federal employment. Details about many of the books and other resources I'll mention are listed at the end of this chapter. Basically, you need a job search strategy that includes four major steps:

- Get Information
- Develop a Job Search Strategic Plan
- Apply for Jobs
- Keep Good Records and Say Thank You

Get Information

Your first step is to get preliminary information on federal agencies, kinds of work, job announcements, and hiring practices. Here are some ideas.

Personal Computer

If you have a modem and communications software on your PC at home, school, or work, you can tap into a wealth of information about jobs and job vacancies. The Office of Personnel Management has a free electronic bulletin board with federal personnel information called MainStreet (202) 606-4800. It has a variety of "forums" for online information and discussion. See also "Federal Job Information is Online" in Chapter 3. You'll also want to consult *Electronic Job Search Revolution* by Joyce Lain Kennedy and Thomas J. Morrow. This wonderful, plain English, forward-thinking resource directory includes electronic job search tools available right now in the federal government.

If you are an Internet user, you can start up Gopher and move around looking for menus and information. I would be more specific, but every time I'm on the Net I seem to wander off in a different direction. The person to go to for help is Dennis V. Damp, the author of *The Book of U.S. Government Jobs* (a super book on job search strategies just chock full of information). He is writing for and managing the new Federal Career Employment Opportunities area within the America Online Career Center. He plans to update federal career information on the service's electronic information boards. Job seekers can schedule appointments on these services with Mr. Damp or leave email messages for him (ddamp@aol.com).

Mr. Damp is also the author of *Health Care Job Explosion! Careers in the 90's*. He writes for MedSearch America, an Internet-allied health job search board. If you have Internet, you can reach MedSearch with these commands:

gopher gopher.medsearch.com9001
For Mosaic users, it's:
hhtp//www.medsearch.com:9001

Users can also have access to the Internet gopher by looking at "All the Gophers in the world," Gopher jewels, Yanoffs list, or links to many healthcare-related gophers.

Daniel Lauber, author of *Government Job Finder* and similar, fact-filled books for the profit and non-profit sectors, has developed database software based on his books that is so reasonably priced it's attractive to the home PC user. Called *Ultimate Job Finder*, it features thousands of the best job leads that you can easily search in your career field.

Libraries and Bookstores

If you still like to get information the traditional way, don't neglect printed books and directories. Learn about the federal government by reviewing the career resources in your school or public library. Many libraries are also adding online career information services.

About 1,400 public and university libraries nationwide are designated federal depository libraries. These libraries get copies of all the major publications of the federal government, some of which are also published on alternate technologies like CD-ROM. Your local library system should be able to tell you the name of the nearest depository library. If you want to get the official information on the new federal hiring processes, you can find it at a depository library. Ask for the December 16, 1994 *Federal Register*, then look on pages 65086-65102.

If you want to get the official information on the new federal hiring processes, you can find it at a depository library.

You can also buy this document and any of 12,000 other government publications, periodicals, and electronic products by going to a U.S. Government Bookstore or calling (202) 512-1800. The bookstores are in Atlanta, Birmingham, Boston, Chicago, Cleveland (OH), Columbus (OH), Dallas, Denver, Detroit, Houston, Jacksonville, Kansas City (MO), Laurel (MD), Los Angeles, Milwaukee, New York, Philadelphia, Pittsburgh, Portland (OR), Pueblo (CO), San Francisco, Seattle, and Washington (DC). Although these bookstores don't carry every title, they are likely to have the publications that I mention in this book. If they don't, they will order it for you.

One of my favorite government publications is *The United States Government Manual*. This comprehensive, authoritative source gives a brief description of every federal agency, including its mission, history, and programs. You will be able to locate the bureaus, divisions, services, offices, and departments that may have career opportunities in your field, complete with names and phone numbers of chief officials in Washington, DC, regional centers and some field sites all over the country. Another excellent government publication is the *Federal Careers Directory*. Although it is out of print, you may be able to find it in a library or career center. This directory explains the types of jobs in the major federal agencies, which is still helpful, and names contact people, but this list is dated. If you have a special career field, you should read about those agencies or offices whose work is compatible with your interests, education, and skills.

There are a plethora of good books on federal employment published in the last 10 years, and many authors are scrambling to update their publications or come out with new titles to reflect the new federal hiring practices. Consider the excellent books written or published by Dennis V. Damp, Ronald L. and Caryl Rae Krannich, and Daniel Lauber, all of whom have their own publishing houses.

Federal Employment Information Centers

If you live in an area with a Federal Employment Information Center, call or stop by. A list of centers is in the Appendices. It's best to stop by so you can use the new job information touch screen computer discussed in Chapter 3. You can also ask for handouts on special topics like student employment, overseas jobs, and other subjects that may interest you. The centers give written tests when they are required, such as typing tests, and they also offer special seminars on federal employment for the general public, veterans, and students. These centers got bad marks on customer service in a 1992 General Accounting Office report, but the Office of Personnel Management is currently improving its information to job hunters as part of its reinventing government initiative.

Phone and Other Directories

Any town with a post office, airport, extension service, VA hospital, or social security office has federal employees. Consult the local phone directory or check the library, which may have phone directories from other cities. Federal agencies will either be in the white pages under US Government or in blue pages for local, state, and federal government offices. You will usually find phone numbers and addresses for personnel offices (which manage the hiring process) and program offices (which have the jobs). You can also buy some federal agency telephone directories from the Government Printing Office. See the resources at the end of this chapter.

There are also two super directories of key officials in the government: the *Federal Yellow Book* and the *Federal Staff Directory*. The latter book, for example, provides the names, addresses, and phone numbers of 32,000 key officials in the executive branch throughout the country. Look them over in the library or career counseling center.

Job Vacancy Subscriptions

You may wish to subscribe to a private newsletter, such as *Federal Career Opportunities* published by Federal Research Service, Inc. or *Federal Jobs Digest* published by Breakthrough Publications. These publications carry thousands of "mini" federal job announcements and supply current job-hunting advice in each issue.

Personal Contacts

Call and visit federal personnel offices, public information offices, and program offices to get advice, information, and job leads. Personnel specialists will know what jobs are posted (announced) and may tell you the names of the persons who will do the actual hiring. It helps if you can be referred by someone (that's why networking is so important), but it's perfectly okay to make cold calls to people whose names you get from directories like the *Federal Yellow Book*.

It's okay to make cold calls to people whose names you get from directories.

Good times to call are early in the day or late in the afternoon when you may have a chance to talk with federal managers without reaching their secretary or voice mail. Jot down what you want to say in advance so you will be professional and concise. Ask the person if this is a good time to call or if you should call again later. Tell the person of your interest in his or her agency and that you would like to visit to get more information about the programs and job opportunities. Public information officers, for example, can give you numerous pamphlets about the agency and its programs, and refer you to program managers in your specific fields.

Let these calls and visits go wherever they lead. You may be making valuable contacts for the future, as well as the present. If it seems appropriate in a phone call, offer to send your resume. (This would be a short generic resume, not one tailored to an announced job. See Chapter 6.) When you visit, leave a copy of a resume or Optional Form 612 if it seems to fit the jobs you've discussed. I have had a lot of success with telephone contacts in both government and the private sector. Most people are friendly and receptive. However, the person may have been working on a tight deadline, and your call was a major interruption. If you sense a negative attitude, say thank you and move on. Don't be concerned about being rejected; it's part of the successful job-hunting process. Most federal managers appreciate learning about capable, resourceful people who have the initiative to make these kinds of calls and visits. Good managers file the resumes of such people who look promising to them, even if they have no immediate openings. Follow up these phone conversations and visits with a brief thank you note for the time and information these officials have given you.

Good managers file the resumes of people who look promising to them.

News Media

Keep up with current events. Agencies often announce their plans for major initiatives (which could mean new hires), tell Congress they are understaffed (which could bring additional money to hire), or announce a new or relocated office (again, maybe some new hires).

Of course, with the reinventing government initiative, the Clinton administration has pledged to cut 273,000 jobs by 1999, and the Republican-controlled 104th Congress that took office in January 1995 has pledged further cuts. Agencies and military bases could shut down, which means a reduction in civilian employees in that area, or there could be a hiring freeze in several agencies or even nationwide, which means a reduction-in-force (RIF). Even with hiring freezes and RIFs, the government is so big that jobs will be open in some agencies and some locations at the same time. Keep up with the news and keep researching.

Develop a Job Search Strategic Plan

As you become familiar with federal job-hunting resources and understand the hiring process and forms, write out the steps you will take to find a federal job. This is a personal job search strategic plan. It should include how and where to gather information as we've just discussed, along with goals and specific tasks, including implementation dates for every activity. Keep revising your plan as you gain new information. Your plan could include these activities:

- Assessing your skills (see Chapter 11)

- Setting up and maintaining a career file

- Getting information on federal agencies and jobs

- Developing contacts and scouting career opportunities

- Interviewing federal officials for information

- Networking in general

- Finding announced job vacancies that fit your skills and interests

- Preparing resumes and application forms

- Applying for jobs

- Following up with the contacts you make

- Keeping good records of your networking and search activities

Note: See the Job Hunting Log at the end of this chapter.

These activities are not sequential. You will do some or all of them at the same time. You can search for a federal job without a written plan, of course. Many people do. Successful job hunters take all or most of these steps, whether they write them down or not.

Apply for Jobs

This section discusses two approaches to applying for federal jobs.

Target the Announced Job

Your computer search, phone calls, visits, research, and/or subscription to a private service should reveal specific job vacancies in your field announced by one or more federal agency. Call the contact person to get a copy of the full job announcement and any supporting documents.

Using the step-by-step instructions in this book, write the experience blocks in your Optional Form 612 or resume around the targeted job. Also prepare a supplemental statement listing each of the selective placement factors or quality ranking factors in the job announcements if this is required.

Send your application package to the personnel office listed on the announcement on or before the closing date. Some, but not all, will accept applications that are postmarked on the closing date, but this is risky. Some agency announcements allow you to fax your application. However, before you fax your resume or forms call to confirm that faxes are accepted. Find out the name of the hiring official, and send your application to that person as well along with a short, informative cover letter. This is a step many applicants fail to do, but it's legal and ethical.

Get Ahead of an Announced Job

These tips are similar to those under "Personal Contacts" in "Get Information" above. The difference is that these contacts are blatantly job-related, and don't beat around the bush about it.

Make a list of government officials by name (associate commissioners, special assistants, office directors, branch chiefs, etc.). Get the names from *The US Government Manual*, the *Federal Yellow Book*, or the *Federal Staff Directory*, or any other source that you might locate in your research. As we've mentioned, if you can get a referral from someone, that's even better.

Verify the accuracy of the name by calling the person's office. In smaller communities you can get the name of the local office from the

Your letter should explain how your skills and experience would help the agency do its work.

phone book and call to get the name of the director. The number of officials on your list will depend upon the number you can handle, a dozen, 25, 100? Send these officials a short, well-written resume with an upbeat cover letter personalized to that agency. Some experts say skip the resume and just send a letter with an attention-getting opener and some of the major points from your resume. Your letter (alone or as a cover) should explain how your skills and experience would help the agency do its work or meet its goals (this is where your research is important). Ask for an interview and say that you will call the office later.

This approach does not work with the highest level government officials like Secretaries, Assistant Secretaries, Commissioners and a few others. These top officials get hundreds of letters from dissatisfied citizens, grant seekers, and a variety of other people every week. They have employees who read and sort their mail and send these letters to program experts who prepare responses. Don't expect personal attention from these high level officials. They may never see your letter. Your best bet is to write bureau chiefs, division heads, and office directors who usually open their own mail and answer their own phones. You will probably get a nibble from only two or three people even if you contact 50. Be sure to make the follow up call. If you get a response, pursue it vigorously. The official may already be thinking about certain kinds of jobs that need to be done. Your letter may have clarified his or her thinking. You may even get a lead on future or current job announcements!

Now back to those top-level officials in Washington, DC. I'm not advising you not to contact these people, just not to write a letter or call as your opener, even if you want a political appointment. The trick here is to get these officials to suggest that you write or call them. This is where networking comes in. If you know someone who knows someone, ask that  person to contact the official on your behalf (formally as in a phone call or informally as at a reception or office function) and pass the response back to you. If you get favorable feedback, you can act accordingly. If the Commissioner has suggested that you call (even through a third person), you should say so and your call is more likely to go through. Likewise, say you are writing at the Commissioner's request, and your letter is more likely to get closer attention.

Keep Good Records and Say Thank You

Finally, keep good records of your job search efforts, including informal contacts and applications for specific jobs. Keep a log with the agency name, announcement number, names and phone numbers for personnel specialist and manager who will make the hiring decision, dates contacted, and follow-up calls and letters including thank you notes. Photocopy the Job Hunting Log in this chapter, or make one to suit your needs.

Also make sure that your application packages are clearly written, well formatted, and professionally presented. You'll find a checklist after the job hunting log.

If You Are a Federal Employee

If you are already a federal employee, you may think the above job hunting tips don't apply to you. This isn't so. Government is changing, and you can no longer expect routine promotions in certain career ladders in your agency as in the past. You're in the best place of all to get information about job vacancies and what's going on in government. If you wish, you can look for jobs in your own agencies or in other agencies anywhere in the country or even in the world. You can have a personal development plan, consultation with personnel counselors within government, an open door to many federal managers, and access to all kinds of job information in the personnel office or agency library. You can try for exciting lateral transfers and details at your own grade level all over government, usually without competing with others. You can locate and suggest these opportunities to your current and prospective supervisor. If they agree, this kind of sideways mobility can be exciting and challenging.

As a known achiever, you have an edge when you apply for a job.

As you compete for promotional opportunities in your own agency, strive for high quality, customer-focused accomplishments, have a positive attitude and be willing to go the extra mile in your current position. These qualities not only bring you to the attention of your supervisor, but also to other managers. As a known achiever, you have an edge when you apply for a job and your name appears on the list of highly qualified candidates. See Chapter 11 for a few more tips to federal employees.

Job Hunting Log

Agency	Contact Person(s) and Phone Number(s)	Announcement Name and Number or Nature of Contact	Date	Agency Response/Follow-Up Needed

Checklist for Your Federal Application Package

This checklist applies to the Optional Form 612, resume, or the Standard Form SF-171.

❑ Neatly typed or word processed with no smudges or typos.

❑ Printed on good quality bond paper in white, cream, or neutral shade.

❑ Completely but concisely written to the requirements of the announced job.

❑ Includes all information requested on the job announcement, *Applying for a Federal Job* flyer, or any other instructions from the agency. **Double check**.

❑ Experience on Optional Form or SF-171 includes paid and nonpaid experience and is organized in way that best highlights your qualifications, usually reverse chronological order. Everything is customized to the job sought.

❑ Experience, education, training, and special skills sections of Optional Form or SF-171 expanded to fit material, avoiding use of clumsy attachment sheets. Everything is customized to the job sought.

❑ Supplementary Qualifications Statement attached to address rating factors (if announcement requires or suggests this statement).

❑ Veterans' Preference, performance appraisals, and other documents attached if requested.

❑ Your name and social security number is at the top of every continuation sheet or attachment.

❑ Unnecessary attachments are discarded (Don't include copies of training certificates, letters, diplomas, etc.).

❑ Optional Form 612 or SF-171 is signed and dated before closing date on job announcement. (You don't have to sign a resume.)

❑ Topped by a short cover letter and/or one-page summary resume (optional, but effective technique).

❑ Application is reviewed by a friend or colleague who will critique impact and presentation.

❑ Unfolded, ready for mailing or delivering personally on or before deadline, in large envelope to personnel office.

❑ Identical package, with cover letter, prepared for selecting official.

❑ Adequate postage. (Federal employees: Do not use government postage to mail applications.)

❑ Electronic and paper copies kept for career file.

Federal Job Resources

Here is a list of books and software to help you learn about federal job vacancies, the federal hiring system, how to assess your skills, how to develop a job search strategy, and other subjects. A number of the books and computer software programs listed in this chapter are available from the publisher's Career Resource Catalog in the back of this book. You may also request catalogs from these publishers: Bookhaven Press, (412) 262-5578; Impact Publications, (703) 361-7300; Planning / Communications, (708) 366-5200.

Software and Online Resources

Access...Federal Career Opportunities On-Line. Thousands of up-to-date federal job openings compiled by Federal Research Service, Inc. Available by hourly subscription ($45 an hour) on any IBM-compatible PC with a 2400 baud Hayes compatible modem. For information, call (703) 281-0200.

Federal Occupational and Career Information System (FOCIS). Developed by the Office of Personnel Management to help job seekers. This PC-based software provides general information about federal careers, occupations, agencies, and training opportunities. It can also help you assess your job interests and skills. Inexpensively priced, this package is available to colleges, career guidance counselors, federal agencies and others, but not every organization has it yet. Order from National Technical Information Services, 5285, Springfield, VA 22161, (800) 553-NTIS or (703) 487-4650.

Quick and Easy Federal Job Application Kit. This Windows 3.1 compatible system by DataTech Software offers an excellent and comprehensive set of tools for obtaining a federal job. It includes the **new optional forms**, the **original SF-171 application**, and it **generates resumes** from data that you entered on your forms. The program is completely menu driven with advanced help at the touch of a button. It includes a word processor with spell check capabilities designed to fill in and manage the new optional forms, **RESUME**, and the original SF-171. This package includes a condensed version of *The Book of U.S. Government Jobs* that can easily be searched with key word commands to locate information at the touch of a button. This program is available from the publisher's back-of-book catalog.

Federal Job Announcements

Federal Career Opportunities (Biweekly job listing), Federal Research Service, P.O. Box 1059-W, Vienna, VA 22183-1059, (800) 822-5627 (outside D.C. area), (703) 281-0200. Contains thousands of federal job listings, GS-5 through

Senior Executive Service. VISA and MasterCard. Subscription rates: $39 - 6 issues; $77 - 12 issues; $175 - 26 issues. An electronic version is also available. See above.

Federal Jobs Digest (Biweekly job listing), Breakthrough Publications, P.O. Box 594, Millwood, NY 10546, (800) 824-5000, (914) 762-5111. Contains thousands of General Schedule and Wage Grade job listings, including display ads. Rates: $29 - 3 mo.; $54 - 6 mo.; $110 - 12 mo. Major credit cards or COD orders.

> Breakthrough Publications also offers a **Federal Job Matching Service**. Applicant provides qualifications on a questionnaire; the company provides applicant with a list of federal job titles and grade levels (with job descriptions and published qualifications) that match his or her qualifications.

National and Federal Legal Employment Report (monthly). A listing of attorney and law-related jobs with the federal government and other public employers in Washington, DC, nationwide and abroad. 1010 Vermont Ave., NW, Suite 408, Washington, DC 20005, (800) 296-9611 or (202) 393-3311. Rates: $39 - 3 mo.; $69 - 6 mo.; $125 - 12 mo.

The Federal Times (a newspaper), 6883 Commercial Dr., Springfield, VA 22159, (800) 368-5718 or (703) 750-7400. Subscription rates: $26 - 6 mo; $48 - 1 yr; $88 - 2 yrs.

You will also find ads for federal professional and technical positions in the business section of *The Washington Post, USA Today, The Wall Street Journal,* and *The New York Times.* You may also find ads for federal jobs in some local newspapers.

Books on Self Assessment, Career Planning, and Federal Hiring

Baxter, Neal, *Opportunities in Federal Government Careers,* 1992, VGB Career Horizons (NTC Publishing Group), Lincolnwood, IL. A guide to federal jobs and organizations.

Bautisa, Veltisezar B., *The Book of U.S. Postal Exams: How to Score 95-100% and Get a $20,000-a-Year Job.* This guide includes the most commonly-given exams for the majority of job classifications. Available from the publisher's back-of-book catalog.

Bolles, Richard Nelson, *What Color Is Your Parachute?*, 1993, Ten Speed Press, P.O. Box 7123, Berkeley, CA, 94707. A perennial best seller by one of the best known career counselors in the country.

Cantrell, Will, and Modderno, Francine, *How to Find an Overseas Job with the Federal Government*, 1992, Worldwise Books. The only book on this specialized area. It's hard to locate, but you can order a copy from the publisher's back-of-book catalog.

Damp, Dennis V., *The Book of U.S. Government Jobs*, 1995, Bookhaven Press, 401 Amherst Ave., Moon Township, PA 15108, (412) 262-5578. An outstanding guide to where federal jobs are and how to get one. Available from the publisher's back-of-book catalog.

Federal Yellow Book, published several times a year, Monitor Leadership Directories, Inc., Second Floor, 104 Fifth Ave., New York, NY 10114-0233, (212) 627-4140. This reference book provides the name, address and phone number of every major official in the federal government. Look for it in a career information center or the public library.

Guide to Federal Technical, Trades and Labor Jobs, 1992, Resource Directories, Suite 301, 3361 Executive Parkway, Toledo, OH 43606, (800) 274-8515. This may be the only reference book that specializes in blue collar and non-professional federal jobs that do not require a college degree.

Guide to Federal Jobs, 1992, Resource Directories, Suite 302, 3361 Executive Parkway, Toledo, OH 43606, (800) 274-8515.

Irish, Richard, *Go Hire Yourself an Employer*, 1987, Anchor Books, Garden City, NY. This is one of my favorite books on job-hunting strategy in any sector.

Jackson, Tom, *Mastering the Hidden Job Market: How to Create Job Opportunities in a World of Uncertainty and Change*, 1992, Random House, New York. A timely book considering the uncertainty of the job market in the 1990s. Focuses on finding a job before it's on the market.

Jackson, Tom, *Not Just Another Job: How to Invent a Career That Works for You—Now and in the Future*, 1992, Times Books, New York.

Kennedy, Joyce Lain, and Morrow, Thomas J., *Electronic Job Search Revolution, Win with the New Technology That's Reshaping Today's Job Market*, 1994, John Wiley & Sons, Inc., New York. These well-known authors tell us that the job search tools of the future are already here.

Kennedy, Joyce Lain, *Joyce Lain Kennedy's Career Book*, 1992, VGM Career Horizons (NTC Publishing Group), IL. A highly-acclaimed guide for beginning job seekers.

Krannich, Ronald L. and Caryl Rae, *The Almanac of American Government Jobs and Careers*, 1991, Impact Publications. Comprehensive information about every office in the three branches of government, including personnel contacts. Available from the publisher's back-of-book catalog.

Krannich, Ronald L. and Caryl Rae, *The Complete Guide to Public Employment*, 1995, Impact Publications. Called the "seminal book on public employment." Available from the publisher's back-of-book catalog.

KSA Workbook, Federal Research Service, P.O. Box 1059, Vienna, VA 22183-1059, (703) 281-0200. A 48-page guide to presenting your knowledge, skills and abilities as a supplement to your federal application.

Lauber, Daniel, *Government Job Finder*. Introduces readers to over 1,400 sources of vacancies for professional, labor, trade, technical, and office staff in local, state, and federal government in the U.S. and overseas. Available from the publisher's back-of-book catalog.

Lauber, Daniel, *Non-Profits' Job Finder*. Introduces readers to over 1,100 sources of jobs, internships, and grant opportunities in the non-profit field: education, teaching, social services, and many other fields. Available from the publisher's back-of-book catalog.

Lauber, Daniel, *Professional's Job Finder*. You'll learn how to use over 2,000 of the best sources to find job vacancies in all aspects of the private sector: health care, science, and engineering, media, computers, manufacturing , law, management, business, banking, and dozens of other fields. Available from the publisher's back-of-book catalog.

Leeds, Dorothy, *Marketing Yourself: The Ultimate Job Seeker's Guide*, 1991, Harper Collins Publishers, New York. This book teaches how to sell yourself to get the job you want.

Moore, Donna (with Susan VanderWey), *Take Charge of Your Own Career. A Guide to Federal Employment*, 1994, Psychological Assessment Resources, Inc. Odessa, FL 33556. This comprehensive book covers the major elements in planning and pursuing a federal career, including discovering your skills, finding out who needs these skills, and marketing yourself to federal organizations.

New Internships in the Federal Government, Graduate Group, 86 Norwood Rd., West Hartford, CT 06117, (203) 232-3100.

Smith, Russ, Ph.D. *Federal Jobs in Law Enforcement*, 1995. Outlines job opportunities in more than 70 agencies requiring law enforcement expertise, Includes FBI, DEA, many others. Available from the publisher's back-of-book catalog.

Smith, Russ, Ph.D. *Federal Jobs in Nursing & Medical Science*, 1995. This book outlines opportunities with various agencies as well as provides application and hiring tips. Available from the publisher's back-of-book catalog.

Smith, Russ, Ph.D. *Federal Jobs in Office Administration*, 1995. Office occupations constitutes one of the largest occupational groupings in the federal government. This book outlines useful application and hiring tips. Available from the publisher's back-of-book catalog.

Smith, Russ, Ph.D. *Federal Jobs in Secret Operations,* Outlines opportunities with the major intelligence services such as the CIA, Defense Intelligence Agency, and the National Security Agency. Includes application and hiring tips. Available from the publisher's back-of-book catalog.

Sutherland, Linda, and Herman, Richard, *The 110 Biggest Mistakes Job Hunters Make (And How to Avoid Them)*, 1994, Federal Reports, Inc., 1010 Vermont Ave., NW, Suite 408, Washington, DC 20005, (202) 393-3311.

Tieger, Paul and Barbara, *Do What You Are: Discover the Perfect Career for You Through the Secrets of Personality Type*, 1992, Little, Brown and Co., Boston. I'm a true believer in the Myers-Briggs Type Indicator. This book explains how to use the principles of personality type to find the career for you.

Wood, Patricia B., *Applying for Federal Jobs: A Guide to Writing Successful Applications and Resumes for the Job You Want in Government*, 1995. Bookhaven Press, 401 Amherst Ave., Moon Township, PA 15108, (412) 262-5578. Available from the publisher's back-of-book catalog.

Wood, Patricia B., *The 171 Reference Book, New Edition*, 1991. The SF-171 can still be used to apply for a federal job. This book has step-by-step instructions and tips galore. Order from Workbooks, Inc., 9039 Sligo Creek Parkway, #316, Silver Spring, MD 20901-3347, phone/fax (301) 565-9467. Discounted at $12.95 plus postage and handling.

Wood, Patricia B., *The 171 Writing Portfolio, Latest Edition*, 1990. Order from Workbooks, Inc., address above. Discounted at $9.95 plus postage and handling.

Wood, Patricia B., *Promote Yourself! How to Use Your Knowledge, Skills and Abilities...and Advance in the Federal Government*, 1988. A helpful guide that gives tips for writing Supplemental Qualifications Statements. Order from Workbooks, Inc., address above. Discounted at $12.95 plus postage and handling.

Resumes

Good books on traditional resumes abound. Check the library or bookstore. Professional resume services may not know much yet about the requirements of a federal style resume. One company that does is **The Resume Place, Inc.**, 1825 K St., NW, Suite 706, Washington, DC 20006, (202) 737-8637.

Publications and Electronic Products From the Federal Government

Government publications and electronic products may be purchased from US Government Book Stores all over the country. Or you may write: The Superintendent of Documents, United States Government Printing Office, Washington, DC 20402-9325. To order books, or get information about available titles, call the Publications Desk, (202) 512-1800. Major credit cards are accepted.

Federal Agency Telephone Directories. These comprehensive telephone directories can help you unravel the thousands of bureaus, divisions, services, offices, and departments of the federal government you may wish to contact about employment opportunities. Directories for many agencies such as the Federal Aviation Administration (S/N 024-000-00806-8), the Department of State (List ID DSTD), and the Department of Defense (List

ID TDD) are available from the Government Printing Office with prices ranging from $5 to $28.

Guide to SES Qualifications, (SES-94-01/August 1994). A valuable road map to writing your qualifications to apply for Senior Executive Service positions. U.S. Office of Personnel Management, Office of Executive Resources, 1900 E St., NW, Room 6464, Washington, DC 20415-0001.

Handbook of Occupational Groups and Series, 1993. Contains grade numbers, titles and descriptions for about 500 positions in the federal civil service. $3.75 (SN 006-000-01385-6).

U.S. Department of Labor's 1994-95 Occupational Outlook Handbook (published every 2 years). This is the basic resource for anyone wanting to know about a particular occupation and is one of the best-selling federal publications. It accounts for the vast majority of the jobs in the country, with detailed information about entry requirements, employment prospects, and other subjects. Order from the Government Printing Office.

Occupational Outlook Quarterly, United States Dept. of Labor, Bureau of Labor Statistics, Washington, DC 20402. Yearly subscription (SN 729-008-00000-1) available from the Government Printing Office.

United States Government Manual, 1993-94, published annually by the General Services Administration. A valuable 943-page reference book that provides the purpose of each federal agency and the names and addresses of major officials all over the country. Order from the Government Printing Office (SN 069-000-00053-3). Also available on the Federal Bulletin Board. Dial (202) 512-1387 with modem (settings 8N1, fwh duplex), telecommunications software and telephone line or Telnet through Internet to Federal.bbs.gpo.gov 3001 (Port 3001), 7 days a week, 24 hours a day.

Free fact sheets for Veterans: *Veterans' Re-Employment Rights Statute*, *Re-Employment Rights for Returning Veterans*, and *Job Rights for Reservists and Members of the National Guard*. Write or call the Veterans Employment and Training Services, Department of Labor, Washington, DC 20210, (202) 219-9110.

Chapter Nine
Student and Entry
Level Positions

The good news for college graduates of any age is that you apply for entry level federal jobs in individual agencies like everybody else. Of course, you've been able to do that for years, but many graduates and soon-to-be graduates didn't know it. Thousands of college students and graduates who wanted a federal career in public service took a written test under a recruitment program called Administrative Careers With America (ACWA) administered by the Office of Personnel Management. That test died in 1994 as part of the reinventing government initiative.

Why the ACWA Test Was Abolished

The ACWA written test, begun in 1990 to recruit for more than 100 professional and administrative occupations at the GS-5 and GS-7 grade levels, was open to those with a college degree or anyone with 3 years of experience without a college education. It was only given at certain times as announced by the Office of Personnel Management.

Passing the test put the applicant on central registers according to occupational groupings, with veterans getting bonus points. Agencies could select from the top applicants on a register, the Office of Personnel Management sent agencies the applicants' "certifications," but the agency still had to take several weeks (or longer) to contact the candidates, review their resumes and paper applications, interview them, and verify their work experience and schooling in order to hire them. So, who needed a test?

So, who needed a test?

Agencies Didn't Use ACWA to Hire

The General Accounting Office evaluated the program and found that federal agencies generally weren't using the test to hire. GAO said that for Fiscal Years 1991 and 1992, agencies filled about 2,800 vacancies through ACWA, but they filled more than 19,000 vacancies through other procedures rather than going to the ACWA central register. And still another 15,000 vacancies were filled internally with promotions, lateral transfers, and other means. Apparently agencies didn't need the test as a recruitment tool.

Students Were Frustrated

But the greatest frustration with the test must have been experienced by the applicants themselves, usually college seniors and recent graduates. GAO found that most applicants were frustrated with the test because they got very little information from the Office of Personnel Management other than their test scores. In response to the GAO questionnaire, 63 percent thought their chances of getting federal jobs were outstanding or good based on their scores. What students didn't know was that from July 1, 1990 through December 31, 1992, ACWA tested more than 300,000 applicants and more than 182,000 passed. Of that number, only slightly more than 3,000 were hired. In May 1994, according to the Office of Personnel Management, the test was closed to any new applicants. At that time 46,000 eligible candidates were on the registers, but only 439 hires were made in 1993. By that time OPM was making an effort to let applicants know how many eligibles were on the central registers, what the average test scores were, how few people were actually hired, and what types of jobs and locations offered the best opportunities.

College Career Counselors Were Frustrated Too

College career counselors were also not enamored of the test. Samantha Stainburn, in an article written for the July 1994 *Government Executive*, quoted the director of career services at Harvard's Kennedy School of Government as saying, "In the 13 years that I've worked here, I've never known a student to get a job off the register." The writer also quoted a graduate-turned-federal-employee as saying, "I'm convinced that networking—using contacts from your college, your fraternity or sorority, even your state—is about the only way to get a job in government."

In November 1994, OPM said the test was a barrier to federal hiring at the entry level professional and administrative occupations and announced it was eliminating the test to fulfill another recommendation of the Clinton Administration's National Performance Review. It also announced computer-scannable questionnaires (see Chapter 3).

To repeat the primary message: College graduates of any age apply for specific, announced job vacancies in federal agencies in any location like any other job seeker. All the tips in this book about finding a job and preparing an application apply to you. Be sure to see the student experience samples in Chapter 4.

Outstanding Scholar Program

If you've got top grades, however, you do have an ace. Try the Outstanding Scholar Program. To qualify, you must be a college graduate with a cumulative grade point average (GPA) of 3.5 or above (on a 4.0 scale) for all undergraduate course work or have graduated in the upper 10 percent of your class or major university subdivision. This program doesn't apply to graduate students.

If you've got top grades, however, you do have an ace.

You may apply directly to any federal agency for any of their announced jobs, assuming you meet the qualifying requirements. You must submit an application as directed by the agency (Optional Form 612, a resume, or the SF-171) and, since your eligibility is based on scholastic achievement, a transcript or OPM Form 1170/17, List of College Courses and Certificate of Scholastic Achievement.

Federal Job Samplers

One of the best ways for students to sample the federal workplace (and get a head start on permanent employment) is to become an intern (with or without school credit and with or without pay) or to work for pay in a part-time or short term student program. In 1993, about 56,000 students were employed at some time by the federal government in a paying job under a number of programs like Stay-In-School, Cooperative Education and Summer Employment.

These programs don't exist anymore, at least not with those names. These programs and others, as part of reinventing government, have been consolidated, simplified, and streamlined. In December 1994, the Office of Personnel Management announced one program, the Student Educational Employment Program.

Student Educational Employment Program

The new Student Educational Employment Program has two parts:

❶   the Student Temporary Employment Program, and
❷   the Student Career Experience Program.

You may be hired under these programs if you are working at least half-time for a:

- high school diploma or general equivalency diploma (GED),
- vocational or technical school certificate, or
- degree (associate, baccalaureate, graduate or professional).

These are year-round programs, and you can be hired at any time during the year, including summer. You may work in the same agency as a parent or other relative, so long as the relative doesn't have anything to do with hiring or supervising you. You can be hired if you are not a citizen, although you must be a citizen if you later convert without competition from the Career Experience Program to a career or career-conditional job. In both the temporary and career experience programs you earn annual and sick leave, can get training paid for by the agency, and are eligible for promotion. The two programs have no special provisions for low-income students, although federal agencies may use financial need as an employment criteria if they wish.

Student Temporary Employment Program

You can be hired for one year under the Student Temporary Employment Program, but the agency can extend the appointment in one-year increments as long as you remain in school. The duties of this temporary job do not have to be related to your career goals or academic studies, although the agency can convert you from the temporary program to the career experience program if your job functions match your educational pursuits. As long as you are in the temporary program, you can't be converted non-competitively to a career or career-conditional job. That doesn't mean you can't get the job, you just have to compete for it and demonstrate in your application that you have the qualifying credentials.

Student Career Experience Program

In this program, your employment will be directly related to your educational program and career goals. This program is modeled after the very successful Cooperative Education Program that no longer exists. You, the federal agency and your school work closely to set up a program that combines work experience and school attendance. The agency can even pay your travel expenses as you commute between school and work.

You are subject to all the conditions governing career or career-conditional employment (which means that your qualifications and suitability for federal employment are evaluated to get you into the program). Thus, you can convert without competition into a career or career-conditional job when you get your diploma, certificate or degree, or when you've worked 640 hours, or otherwise met the qualification standards for the job you or the agency have targeted. This is no guarantee of a job, of course, but it's pretty certain if the agency wants you and it's not reducing its workforce.

How to Find Student Programs

The best way to find out if federal agencies near your home or school are using the Student Educational Employment Program is to contact their personnel offices as we discussed in Chapter 8. You may also use the resources we discussed in Chapter 3: the Career America Connection at (912) 757-3000, the Federal Job Information Touch Screen Computers at various locations, and online on the Federal Job Information Opportunities Board at (912) 757-3100. Remember, post office jobs are not included in these listings since the U.S. Postal Service, as an excepted agency, has a separate competitive system. Check with the local post office. See Dennis V. Damp's *The Book of U.S. Government Jobs* and other resources listings in Chapter 8.

Other excepted agencies may also have student programs. One example is the Central Intelligence Agency. At the CIA you could get exposed to coded messages and foreign languages, providing you qualify. The CIA can be reached at P.O. Box 12727, Arlington, VA 22209, (703) 482-7411. Check the phone books and directories mentioned in Chapter 8 resources, and look at the list of excepted agencies in the Appendices.

Other Student Opportunities

You may find other opportunities if you look. And, "formal" program or not, some federal managers may be able to work with the personnel office to bring you on board for either a paid or nonpaid work experience as an intern. Some of my best student workers were interns who got school credit and lots of experience, but no money. With the reinventing government underway, agencies are encouraged to "partner" with businesses, schools, and non-profit organizations to find ways of cutting bureaucratic red tape and improve service to the public. This is the best time I've ever seen for government and its many constituencies to find new ways of doing business, including mutually beneficial student internships and volunteer programs.

Some of my best student workers were interns who got school credit and lots of experience, but no money.

Getting new intern programs started isn't just the role of a government agency. The initiative can come from the college or university, or even from individuals. In one small, cutting edge federal organization in which I worked, volunteers of all ages sometimes appeared at our door ready to work and learn. Often we were able to take them up on their offer. At other times we were on the phone trying to locate interns or enlist private sector volunteers and advisors in planning conferences, communications projects, and training programs. Almost all of our student interns or volunteers went on to permanent jobs, most of which were in the public sector, based on the contacts they made working with our federal agency!

Of course, not every federal organization or manager has caught on to this new way of relating to the public. But many are exploring these avenues as resources dwindle due to federal employee buyouts and reductions in force (RIFs) to keep the Clinton Administration and Congress's pledge to reduce the size of the government. The agencies need the help; interns get valuable learning experiences that look great on resumes.

Presidential Management Intern (PMI) Program

The Presidential Management Intern Program is by far the most prestigious and competitive of the federal government's entry-level career development and training programs. Designed for outstanding master's and doctoral level students, its purpose is to attract men and women from diverse social and cultural backgrounds who show great promise for public service through their leadership, exceptional ability, and personal commitment to service. Of the approximately 200 federal employees that Vice President Gore assembled to work on the National Performance Review, about 75 were PMI interns who performed brilliantly.

Nominations, Selections, and Placements

You do not apply directly for this program; nominations come from academic institutions. For the class of 1994, OPM, which oversees the program, reported almost 1,200 nominations from more than 230 colleges and universities. Of those nominated, 178 finalists were selected. Qualifying as a PMI finalist makes you eligible for an appointment, but it does not guarantee a job. According to OPM, finalists must follow a course of action similar to competing in the open job market. Placement depends on personal preference for a particular type of position, agency, or geographic location, as well as the special expertise or skills needed by an agency. OPM sponsors a job fair to assist interns and agencies in these placements.

PMI Interns receive 2-year excepted service appointments at a GS-9 level. After the first year is successfully completed, interns are eligible for promotion to a GS-11 salary level. After the 2-year internship, PMIs are eligible for non-competitive conversion to career or career-conditional status and can be promoted to GS-12. See the GS salary schedule in Chapter 2.

The intern placements are not jobs into which you disappear within the huge bureaucracy. The Office of Personnel Management provides a structured career environment through conferences, seminars, briefings, and special programs. PMIs are brought together for these events no matter where they are placed in the country (although many are in the Washington, DC area). In addition, agencies that hire PMIs often offer special orientations and workshops and assign officials as mentors. These structured events help the PMIs get the "big picture" on public issues and managerial concerns. Federal managers regard PMIs as innovative, academically-prepared individuals who are capable of making a significant contribution to the missions of their agencies. In previous years, agencies within big departments like Health and Human Services, NASA, State, Treasury, and Justice have hired the lion's share of PMIs.

Competitive Process and Qualifications

The Office of Personnel Management operates the program on a yearly cycle that begins in September when PMI announcements are mailed to graduate schools over the country. OPM recommends that schools administer a competitive process on its own campus to ensure that all students interested in the program are considered. However, each school may determine its own process for selecting nominees. A school may nominate up to three percent of a graduating class. The intern program does not require the student's course work to have a public sector focus if that interest can be demonstrated in other ways in the application. To be nominated, individuals must be citizens of the United States or expect to receive citizenship status by the date they become interns.

Completing this kind of application is not something you can breeze through in an afternoon.

Graduate students who complete or who expect to complete an advanced degree from an accredited U.S. college or university during an academic year (September 1 - August 31) are eligible to be nominated. Any exceptions to this requirement are considered on a case-by-case basis. Graduate degrees from foreign universities are considered on an individual basis, must be from an accredited program, and be equivalent to those granted by U.S. institutions. For 1995, nominations had to be received by February 1, with finalists selected and notified by March, agencies notified by April, and placements occurring between May and December.

If you are interested in this program, you should start planning early in your graduate career. Nominations must be made by either the appropriate academic dean or department chairperson of your graduate school. Although nominations from individual professors, advisors, or placement counselors are not accepted, these officials can certainly help make your achievements and potential for public service known to the nominating officials. If for some reason you can't get information on this program on your campus (including a look at the application package), call the Career America Connection at (912) 757-3000. Even if the nomination deadline has passed for the 1995 cycle, it would be helpful to see the application package.

How to Write an Application

Even though the appropriate deans write the Presidential Management Intern nomination, they do not write the application. The applicant does. The application form for the 1995 cycle (deadline February 1) includes most of the exact questions found on the abolished Standard Form 171. Thus, the step-by-step instructions in my previous book, *The 171 Reference Book*, would be helpful to any applicant. However, the concepts and tips in this book, *Applying for Federal Jobs*, would be almost as good. The PMI application package also requires the applicant to complete a questionnaire, submit transcripts and evaluations from two persons about your qualifications, and write one-page essays to answer these questions:

- Explain why you are seeking entry to the federal service, describe your career interests, and explain the ways in which you intend to contribute to public service.

- Describe any college, civic, or work activity that demonstrates your ability to work as a team member and how your participation as a member of the team led to the team accomplishing its objective.

- Describe an example of your leadership skills and abilities carried out in the past three years.

- Write a memorandum as though it was going to a director of a government agency, recommending action on a specific issue. Explain why you think the issue is important, the pros and cons of the issue, and why you think the director should support it.

As you can see, completing this kind of application is not something you can breeze through in an afternoon. It will take many hours of preparation and writing, and rightly so, considering the prestige of the internship. I cannot predict whether the application package for the 1996 PMI cycle and subsequent years will continue to use the questions from the abolished SF-171 form or if it will contain questions from the streamlined optional application form we discussed in Chapter 3. My guess is that the 171-type questions will continue as a part of the PMI application, considering the thoroughness of the PMI process and the rigors of the evaluation process, which includes a review by a panel of academicians, federal officials, and non-federal officials.

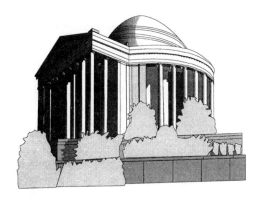

Chapter Ten
Senior Executive Service

This chapter is about applying for the highest paid and most responsible jobs in the executive branch, those held by about 7,800 career and noncareer employees who serve in the key positions just below the top Presidential appointees. Don't skip this chapter even if you're not in the market for these high-level positions. But it is okay to skip a few pages till you reach the part about how candidates write their applications to get appointed to these top jobs. **I consider the writing tips and samples developed for the Senior Executive Service by the Office of Personnel Management to be the model for federal job hunters at every grade level in every occupational field.**

Don't skip this chapter even if you're not in the market for these high-level positions.

What Is the Senior Executive Service?

The Senior Executive Service is a separate personnel and pay system that takes over where the General Schedule positions up to GS-15 end. By law, SES positions are excluded from certain agencies, including the Foreign Service, the Federal Bureau of Investigation, the Drug Enforcement Administration, government corporations, certain financial regulatory agencies, and intelligence agencies. However, some of these agencies have established their own SES-like systems.

The vast majority of positions are filled by career appointees, who must compete for their first appointment to the SES. Up to 10 percent of the positions may be filled by noncareer appointments. These are the political positions controlled by the White House and high level political appointees. These officials are responsible for carrying out Administration policies. However, agencies approve both the technical and managerial qualifications of noncareer appointees. Sometimes, when an agency has to hire more quickly than competitive procedures allow, it may make emergency and limited term appointments. More than 70 percent of SES members are in the Washington, DC area.

An agency must advertise SES vacancies throughout the government, even when it has an ample stock of candidates within its own organization. An agency may also open the vacancy to candidates outside government, and even recruit aggressively if it anticipates any problem with locating qualified candidates. In practice, especially in large agencies, candidates are largely drawn from the pool of competent, qualified GS-15s, some of whom have already gone through developmental programs to prepare themselves to join the highest

Pay Schedules - 4 Senior Executive Service January - 1995	
ES-1	$ 92,900
ES-2	$ 97,400
ES-3	$101,800
ES-4	$107,300
ES-5	$111,800
ES-6	$115,700

executive ranks. Individuals compete to get in such programs and may be hired across agencies without further competition. Veterans' Preference is not a factor in SES hiring. As a whole, SES members are not only experienced, they are well educated. About 68 percent have an educational degree beyond the bachelor's level. Thirty-three percent have a PhD, MD, or JD.

Equity Is Overdue

The representation of women in the SES has more than doubled since 1979, and the representation of minorities has increased since 1987, but the numbers are still dismal. For example, only 9 percent of the members were minorities as of September 1993, according to the Office of Personnel Management.

The Merit Systems Protection Board issued a report in 1992 called *A Question of Equity*. It analyzed gender differences in the federal workforce and made this conclusion: Despite outstanding gains made by women in federal occupations, the "glass ceiling" exists in the federal government as it does in the private sector. Only 12-13 percent of SES positions are held by women, and women make up only 15 percent of the GS-15s--the pool from which SESers are selected. Overall, men are about three grades higher than women. The report thoughtfully considered all the possible reasons that explained this gender gap and came up with several feasible answers. Even so, it theorized that discrimination against women still exists in the federal government, and it's seen when you look at "big picture" figures like these. It's very difficult to see in individual cases, however.

With women expected to make up half the federal workforce by the turn of the century, with less stereotyping of "women's roles," and with candid reports like this, women are almost sure to achieve a fairer share of the upper level jobs in the future—if they work for it. It is, as the Merit System Report suggests, a question of equity—which, after all, is a major intent of the civil service system. Agencies are using candidate development programs to increase the number of female and minority candidates in the Senior Executive Service.

Openings Projected Despite Smaller SES

However, the SES corps is getting smaller and is facing cuts in slots in keeping with the intent of the Clinton Administration and the 104th Congress to reduce the size of the federal workforce. The Department of Defense, with the largest number of SES positions (about 1,400), had 72 fewer members at the end of Fiscal Year 1993 than at the end of FY 1991. However, it still had 18 percent of all SES members. An expected mass exodus of SESers government-wide did not materialize in 1994, possibly because of uncertainties of job opportunities in the business sector. Even so, preliminary data show that more than twice as many career SES members retired between January and June 1994 (more than 660) than during all of the previous year (301). Large percentages of current senior executives are eligible for retirement in the various agencies, opening up the possibility of jobs for employees who are waiting, or for aggressive job seekers from outside government. For example, in projections made by the Office of Personnel Management through the end of 1994, 41 percent of Health and Human Services' 587 career SES members (including Social Security) are eligible for retirement. Fifty-one percent of NASA's 550 senior executives are eligible and 31 percent of Treasury's 533 are eligible. Among smaller agencies, 43 percent of the National Labor Relations Board's 56 SES members are eligible to retire. The percentages range from about 20 to 50 percent in agencies all over government.

Government wide, 32 percent of the career executives in the largest occupational group (administration and management) are eligible for retirement, but the second largest occupational group (the engineering field), could be hardest hit, with 47 percent eligible for retirement and another 33 percent eligible for an early-out.

Senior Executive Service Application Process

Here are the steps in the SES Merit Staffing Process:
1.   Agency advertises position as (a) open to only current federal civil service employees or (b) to all qualified persons, which means that anyone may apply.
2.   Candidates submit their applications to the agency based on the requirements listed in the announcement.
3.   Agency rating panel reviews and ranks candidates.

The "glass ceiling" exists in the federal government as it does in the private sector.

4.   Agency Executive Resources Board recommends list of best qualified candidates to the selecting official.

5.   Selecting official makes a choice and determines that the candidate meets both the technical and managerial (Executive Core) qualifications for the position.

6.   Agency submits papers on the candidate to OPM's Qualifications Review Board, for certification of managerial qualifications.

7.   Agency makes appointment following the Board certification.

How to Find SES Job Vacancies

The Office of Personnel Management publishes *SES Vacancy Announcements* bi-weekly. This listing is available in all agency personnel offices nationwide, as well as state employment offices, and OPM Federal Employment Information Centers. SES openings also appear in private publications such as *Federal Career Opportunities*, *Federal Times*, and *Federal Jobs Digest*, available by subscription and also in many public libraries.

SES vacancy announcements are also online, including six OPM electronic bulletin boards:

Atlanta, GA, (404) 730-2370
Detroit, MI, (313) 226-4423
Los Angeles, CA, (818) 575-6521
Philadelphia, PA, (215) 580-2216
Washington, DC, "PayPerNet," (202) 606-2675 or 1876
Washington, DC, "OPM Mainstreet," (202) 606-4800

SES Qualifications Have Been Reinvented

The 1993 National Performance Review recommended that the Senior Executive Service develop a "corporate perspective" that supports Government-wide cultural change. In that spirit, the Office of Personnel Management surveyed more than 20,000 federal supervisors, managers and executives. Their responses helped shape a Leadership Effectiveness Framework that in turn helped the administrators of the Senior Executive Service update the skills and qualifications that senior executives need to respond to and lead a rapidly changing workplace and workforce. This is important to help the Qualifications Review Board certify the new SES career appointees. It's also important for applicants, who must understand what qualifications they need to be selected as senior executives. These qualifications are called Executive Core Qualifications. Each of the five qualifications has supporting Key Characteristics and Competencies.

Executive Core Qualifications

The ECQs do not include professional, technical, or program knowledge, skills, and abilities (e.g., accounting, engineering, law, natural resources, science), which are covered in the qualifications standards for particular SES positions and will be indicated on a job announcement.

The 1993 National Performance Review recommended that the SES develop a corporate perspective.

1. **Strategic Vision**--The ability to ensure that key national and organizational goals, priorities, values, and other issues are considered in making program decisions, and exercising leadership to implement and to ensure that the organization's mission and strategic vision are reflected in the management of its people.

2. **Human Resources Management**--The ability to design human resource strategies to meet the organization's mission, strategic vision, and goals and to achieve maximum potential of all employees in a fair and equitable manner.

3. **Program Development and Evaluation**--The ability to establish program/policy goals and the structure and processes necessary to implement the organization's mission and strategic vision. Inherent in this process is ensuring that programs and policies are being implemented and adjusted as necessary, that the appropriate results are being achieved, and that a process for continually examining the quality of program activities is in place.

4. **Resources Planning and Management**--The ability to acquire and administer financial, material, and information resources. It also involves the ability to accomplish the organization's mission, support program policy objectives, and promote strategic vision.

5. **Organizational Representation and Liaison**--The ability to explain, advocate, and negotiate with individuals and groups internally and externally. It also involves the ability to develop an expansive professional network with other organizations and organizational units.

Key Characteristics/Leadership Effectiveness Framework Competencies

Key Characteristics are behavioral activities. The Competencies are attributes of an executive who successfully demonstrates the Key Characteristics. For example, a Senior Executive Service candidate may have experience in exercising leadership and motivating managers to incorporate vision, strategic planning, and elements of quality management into an organization's activities (Key Characteristics of ECQ 1, Strategic Vision). In order to accomplish this characteristic successfully, he or she needs to be able to think creatively, to exercise leadership, to be able to plan and evaluate, to use team building techniques, to be vision oriented, etc. (Leadership Effectiveness Framework Competencies associated with Strategic Vision).

Here are the Leadership Effectiveness Framework Competency definitions:

Conflict Management--Anticipates and seeks to resolve confrontations, disagreements, and complaints in a constructive manner.

Creative Thinking--Develops insights and solutions; fosters innovation among others.

Customer Orientation--Actively seeks customer input; ensures customer needs are met; continuously seeks to improve the quality of services, products, and processes.

Decisiveness--Takes action and risks when needed; makes difficult decisions when necessary.

External Awareness--Stays informed on laws, policies, politics, Administration priorities, trends, special interests, and other issues; considers external impact of statements or actions; uses information in decision-making.

Financial Management--Prepares and justifies budget; monitors expenses; manages procurement and contracting.

Flexibility--Adapts to change in the work environment; effectively copes with stress.

Human Resources Management--Ensures effective recruitment, selection, training, performance appraisal, recognition, and corrective/disciplinary action; promotes affirmative employment, good labor relations, and employee well-being.

Influencing/Negotiating--Networks with, and provides information to, key groups and individuals; appropriately uses negotiation, persuasion, and authority in dealing with others to achieve goals.

Interpersonal Skills--Considers and responds appropriately to the needs, feelings, capabilities and interests of others; provides feedback; treats others equitably.

Leadership--Demonstrates and encourages high standards of behavior; adapts leadership style to situations and people; empowers, motivates, and guides others.

Management Controls/Integrity--Ensures the integrity of the organization's processes; promotes ethical and effective practices.

Managing Diverse Workforce--Recognizes the value of cultural, ethnic, gender, and other individual differences; provides employment and development opportunities for a diverse workforce.

Oral Communication--Listens to others; makes clear and effective oral presentations to individuals and groups. (Note: Use of a sign language interpreter may be appropriate for people who are deaf or hard-of-hearing).

Planning and Evaluating--Establishes policies, guidelines, plans, and priorities; identifies required resources; plans and coordinates with others; monitors progress and evaluates outcomes; improves organizational efficiency and effectiveness.

Problem Solving--Recognizes and defines problems; analyzes relevant information; encourages alternative solutions and plans to solve problems.

Self-Direction--Realistically assesses own strengths, weaknesses, and impact on others; seeks feedback from others; works persistently toward a goal; demonstrates self-confidence; invests in self-development; manages own time efficiently.

Team Building--Fosters cooperation, communication, and consensus among groups.

Technical Competence--Demonstrates technical proficiency and an understanding of its impact in areas of responsibility.

Technology Management--Encourages staff to stay informed about new technology; applies new technologies to organizational needs; ensures staff are trained and capable.

Vision--Creates a shared vision of the organization; promotes wide ownership; champions organizational change.

Written Communication--Communicates effectively in writing; reviews and critiques others' writing.

How to Write SES Qualifications Statements

The following instructions and sample (starting at the next paragraph and continuing until the end of this chapter) were taken almost verbatim from *Guide to SES Qualifications*, a lucid, helpful booklet (SES-94-01/August 1994) written for SES candidates and to agency personnel who manage executive resources. It was developed by the Office of Personnel Management's Office of Executive Resources.

Excerpts from Guide to SES Qualifications

Start your qualifications statement with a brief summary of your managerial experience before individually addressing the five Executive Core Qualifications. The key to a well-written qualifications statement is to give your readers—executive resources staff, rating officials, selecting officials, and QRB members—the information they need to compare your experience to the Executive Core Qualifications. Based on discussions with QRB members, we know that the preferred style is short, concise qualifications statements.

An Activities/Context/Outcome Approach

For each ECQ, provide at least one example of your experience. Keep in mind that the QRB will be looking for specific, job-related activities. In addition, they will be interested in the context and outcomes of these activities.

Follow these steps as you document your experience:

- First, identify specific job-related activities (e.g., leadership, planning, acquiring a diverse workforce, budgeting) in which you participated and describe your actions. The Key Characteristics listed under each ECQ provide a guide to the key actions that are relevant to executive jobs.
- Next, describe the context or environment within which you performed these actions. Mention other individuals or groups involved in the activity (e.g., client groups, members or staff of Congress, individuals in other agencies or organizations).

- Finally, state the outcomes of your actions. These indicate the quality and effectiveness of your performance and demonstrate your ability to achieve results, a key requirement of executive positions.

This example illustrates the activities/context/outcomes format:

"I supervised eight professional engineers in the development of a complex technological forecast (**activity**). *It had to be completed very quickly in order for the client company to compete for a major Army contract* (**context**). *The forecast was completed on time, and contracting documents indicated it was a major factor in the company winning the contract* (**outcome**)."

Some Other Suggestions

In addition to the activities/context/outcomes framework, keep these points in mind when writing your qualifications statements:

- You may demonstrate competence in the Executive Core Qualifications through:
    - ✔ regular supervisory/managerial responsibilities;
    - ✔ special assignments, such as task force; or
    - ✔ as a specialist responsible for much of the technical work on a plan, budget, or other project.
- You should cite relevant formal training which enhanced the Executive Core Qualification.
- You may cite relevant, non-federal experience such as work in the private sector and volunteer and professional organizations.

Key Characteristics in Executive Core Qualification 1, Strategic Vision, such as understanding the national policy-making process, exercising leadership, and motivating managers to incorporate vision, strategic planning, and quality management into their organizations, can be demonstrated in a non-federal job. For example, a private sector lawyer might state, "I was responsible for interpreting Securities and Exchange Commission (SEC) and national rules and policies to clients and for advising them about how to design business strategies, services, and applications in compliance with SEC and other regulations, as well as in anticipation of SEC policy trends. I handled a major case for ..."

- You don't need to specifically address each Leadership Effectiveness Framework Competency or Key Characteristic identified in the five Executive Core Qualifications, nor are you expected to be a subject matter expert in all of the Leadership Effectiveness Framework Competencies. However, qualifications statements should contain enough representative examples to provide a sound basis for reviewers to assess the breadth and depth of your executive qualifications.

Writing Sample for Program Development and Evaluation (Executive Core Qualification 3)

The ability to establish program/policy goals and the structure and processes necessary to implement the organization's mission and strategic vision. Inherent in this process is ensuring that programs and policies are being implemented and adjusted as necessary, that the appropriate results are being achieved, and that a process for continually examining the quality of program activities is in place.

Key Characteristics Include:

a.   Assessing policy, program, and project feasibility.
b.   Formulating short- and long-term goals and objectives and integrating them into a strategic plan.
c.   Structuring and organizing work and setting priorities.
d.   Anticipating and identifying, diagnosing, and consulting on potential or actual problem areas relating to program implementation and goal achievement; selecting from alternative courses of corrective action; and/or taking action from developed contingency plans.
e.   Setting effectiveness, efficiency, productivity, evaluation, and management/internal control standards.
f.   Establishing and utilizing procedures and processes to monitor programs toward organizational objectives.
g.   Taking any necessary corrective action to ensure an effective, efficient, and productive organizational unit.

Leadership Effectiveness Framework Competencies

Creative Thinking
Customer Orientation
Decisiveness
External Awareness
Flexibility
Human Resources Management
Influencing/Negotiating
Leadership
Management Controls/Integrity
Oral Communication
Planning & Evaluating
Problem Solving
Self-Direction
Team Building
Technology Management
Vision
Written Communication

Weak Example

"My organization has 176 employees.**1** My responsibilities run the gamut of administrative functions. For example, I have effected major management improvements of my organization's computer capabilities. **2** In addition, I recently completed a detail as Special Assistant to the agency director. I performed staff assignments in all areas of administration, including personnel, budget, management information systems, accounting, and procurement. This assignment gave me a unique overview of many projects. **3** I am closely involved in monitoring ongoing activities, identifying both potential and present deficiencies, and making recommendations for their ultimate improvement and correction. For example, I updated the Agency Program System Plan, a major undertaking." **4**

1. Number of employees supervised is not, in itself, evidence of competence. Additional information is needed to show how this supervision relates to the competencies being addressed.
2. Too general; does not illustrate how or why the candidate effected these improvements.
3. Listing staff assignments does not illustrate specific experience in directing and guiding programs, projects, or policies.
4. Candidate does not define competencies or experience.

Good Example

*"As Director of the Food, Housing, and Recreation Services, I established an aggressive inspection process to focus on quality control and oversee operations at department facilities providing these services.*1 *This resulted in a $10 million increase in authorized appropriated funding, and more efficient operation of our restaurants, troop lodgings, and recreation programs.*2 *The Secretary praised the inspection program as one of the best in the department. One of my initiatives was developing formal staff assistance and oversight teams that visited each base's services to correct problems. I achieved a similar success in another project. I established a Staff Evaluation Team which visited each base and provided guidance on how to improve services.*3 *Civilian restaurants at one base had a loss of over $50,000 in 1991. My team's efforts lead to restaurant profits of $95,000 in 1993.*

Working with the department's Food, Housing, and Recreation Advisory Board, I developed and implemented a strategic planning process which adopted corporate standards as well as the long- and short-range strategies to achieve improvements in these services. These standards were keys to the successes achieved in the Gulf War, and they are still being used to meet our food, housing, and recreational needs at all bases." **4**

1.   Describes an activity -- direction of a major project.
2.   Describes a specific outcome.
3.   Describes the environment.
4.   Example of an effective management control standard.

Chapter Eleven
Get a Vision: How to Plan
or Reinvent Your Federal Career

Socrates was right. "Know thyself" is a most important piece of knowledge. It works for job hunters, especially if you are considering a federal career or are already in the government and hoping for advancement. Whoever you are, whatever you do, you need to know your skills and abilities. You also need to know what you like to do, what you do well, and your weaknesses as well as your strengths.

I'd like to add one corollary for job hunters today: Know thy job market. In today's changing government, it also helps to be flexible, customer-focused, resourceful, and able to communicate and team up with other people in your office, your agency, or across government. To succeed in such an environment, you must be willing to adapt to change and make yourself and your contributions visible in your office and in your agency. Even more, you have to plan and take specific steps. Don't just do a good job for the agency; do a good job for yourself and your career. Understand your own knowledge, skills, abilities, how you work best, what kind of personality you have and how you relate to other people.

Don't just do a good job for the agency; do a good job for yourself and your career.

If you need help, several people have written some good books with chapters on identifying your skills and abilities. One such book is *Take Charge of Your Own Career, A Guide to Federal Employment*, by Donna Moore. It's full of exercises and charts, and other tools to help you know yourself. Other helpful books are Richard N. Boles' perennial best seller, *What Color is Your Parachute?*; *Joyce Lain Kennedy's Career Book*; and any of several books by Drs. Ronald L. and Caryl Rae Krannich. See resources at the end of Chapter 8.

Even if you don't do the exercises, read the books. You'll run into a lot of good word lists to use when you describe yourself and your skills on a resume, Optional Form 612, or the SF-171.

Know Where You Want to Go and Plan How to Get There

I have a colleague—let's call her "Ann"—who went to work for the government as a GS-7 program analyst right out of college at age 22. She had majored in English literature and minored in sociology. She moved up to a GS-12 in less than 5 years and at age 27 she became a GS-13. Two years later she was a GM-14, and the following year, at age 30 she was selected for a prestigious exchange program in business. Next she was selected for a Senior Executive Service developmental program. She quickly moved into a GS-15, and, at age 33, into the Senior Executive Service, the government's highest non-political positions.

She got where she is today because she learned and did well in each job as she went up the ladder, and because she fortified herself at every step of the way with the technical knowledge and training to prepare herself for increasingly responsible executive positions in a changing federal workplace. Ann planned her career, continued learning, and took advantage of every opportunity.

Learn What Successful People Know

Unless you're 22, you probably can't do what Ann did. However, no matter what your age or grade level, you can improve yourself, learn something new, and do an even better job. Maybe even get yourself promoted. It's not too late.

Your road may be very different. I know other people who have gotten ahead in the federal government by very different means. Some didn't go to college. Some were shy. Some were physically handicapped. Some felt discriminated against. But most of them, sooner or later, woke up and started planning where they wanted to go and how they were going to get there. Here are tips from these successful federal workers:

It's a good idea to have a career plan.

- Develop realistic personal goals, based on your own skills and interests, but goals that can change as you learn and grow.
- Understand and be committed to your agency's mission and vision.
- Know your agency's goals and help the agency meet those goals.
- Take advantage of opportunities. Make opportunities for yourself.
- Do the best job you can wherever you are, which usually means doing more than is expected and constantly learning new ways.
- Accept individual responsibility, but be able to work as part of a team.
- Seek training (even if you have to pay for it on your own) and developmental assignments.

It's a good idea to have a career plan. Make a six-month and a five-year plan, with specific steps and activities that incorporate job goals, new skills needed, training ideas, possible developmental assignments, and names of people who can help you plan and act. The main purpose of the six-month plan is to make sure you do something now. If you are going to accomplish something in six months, you have to start today. Don't plan longer than five years. Jobs are changing, the workforce is changing, technology is increasing. Keep your plan flexible enough to change as the world changes.

*S*eek help from college counselors, agency specialists, colleagues, or a mentor.

Seek help from college counselors, career development specialists, colleagues, or a mentor, if you can get one. The Office of Personnel Management has also developed a software package, *Federal Occupational and Career Information System* (FOCIS). PC-based, it helps you get general information about federal careers, occupations, agencies, and training opportunities. It can also help you assess your job interests and skills. Inexpensively priced, this package is available to colleges, career guidance counselors, federal agencies and others, but not every organization has it yet. If you are a federal worker, ask your personnel office if they have it or can get it. If you are outside government call your closest Federal Employment Information Center. These centers are also listed in the Appendices.

Know the Organization and Its Vision

One of the most important things you need to know is the agency's structure, customers, mission, vision, and way of working. You also need to know who heads the agency, how big its budget is, how many employees it has and where they work, and how they measure the results of what they do. Finally, and most important of all, if you are a federal worker, you need to know where you fit in and how your work contributes to what the agency does. If you are not a federal worker, you need to know how your skills will help the agency achieve its mission—something you can make use of in a cover letter.

I developed the following worksheet to help federal employees see the big picture and "reinvent" their own careers. I believe it will help applicants for federal jobs as well. Information from the worksheet will help you scope your job, describe your work, and develop personal goals that help the agency achieve its purpose.

It's an exciting time to enter public service, a time of change for the federal workforce and the institution of government. I hope you achieve your vision, whatever it is, and that you can help government serve better, cost less, and regain the trust of the American people.

Your Agency's Mission and Goals

	Your Agency	Your Division	YOU
Mission/Vision			
Scope (number of employees, size of budget, etc.)			
Special goals, initiatives or priorities	**Reinventing Government**	**Reinventing itself**	**Reinventing yourself and your federal career**
How your job promotes the mission and goals			
What you (and your team) can do to promote your agency's mission and goals			

Chapter Twelve
Speak the Language:
A Federal Hiring Glossary

As a serious job hunter, you must market yourself and your skills in the federal agencies where the jobs are. It will help to know some of the federal hiring jargon, even though these words are changing, with new terms being added and some terms becoming obsolete as the federal hiring process undergoes major change during the 90s. Here are a few common terms to help you get through the maze.

It will help to know some of the federal hiring jargon.

ADMINISTRATIVE CAREERS WITH AMERICA: A program administered by the Office of Personnel Management through which college graduates may apply for entry level professional and administrative jobs. As of November 1994, applicants no longer take written tests as the first step. Applicants complete easy computer-scannable questionnaires; the Office of Personnel Management sends lists of the best qualified applicants to hiring agencies. Entry level applicants apply to agencies for specific jobs (whether they have completed the questionnaire or not). Agencies may require written tests for some types of jobs.

ANNOUNCEMENT: A written notice of a job or a category of jobs for which the public may apply. There are various kinds of announcements. Here are two kinds:

> **Vacancy Announcement**: A written statement or notice of one or more vacant positions published by a federal agency with specific job opening(s). The announcement describes the qualifications required. You apply directly to the federal agency. Normally the agency will rate the applicants and fill the job. In some cases, the agency may ask the Office of Personnel Management to rate and rank the applications of candidates who meet the minimum qualifications. The Office of Personnel Management will then supply the agency with a list of eligible candidates, and the agency will make the selection.

General Notice Announcement: A written notice of a variety of positions published by the Office of Personnel Management for which applications will be accepted for a designated period of time. Sometimes these are hard-to-fill jobs. The Office of Personnel Management will set up registers of eligible candidates from which federal agencies may hire if they have vacancies.

APPOINTMENT: Selection (or hiring) for a federal job. Proposed reforms would simplify this selection to two kinds of appointments--permanent and temporary. Until this change is implemented, here are the types of appointments:

Career-Conditional Appointment: An initial appointment to a federal job in the competitive service that leads to a permanent position after three years of satisfactory service. Your first year is probationary; for the next two years the regulations regarding firing are open and allow the agency flexibility in adjusting employment levels.

Career Appointment: A permanent appointment that occurs automatically after you have completed the career-conditional period.

Temporary Appointment: A job that lasts a year or less, but can be extended for not more than 1 year. At the end of the 2-year period, the position can no longer be considered temporary and cannot be filled by temporary appointment. This rule does not apply to those who work less than 1,040 hours a year.

Term Appointment: A temporary position that allows you to work on a project from 1 to 4 years. You can be promoted or transferred.

If you are a veteran who served during and after the Vietnam era, ask about:

Veterans Readjustment Appointment: A special 2-year appointment for eligible Vietnam-era veterans that waives tests or competition with non-veterans. Successful completion can lead to a permanent appointment. Agencies can use this appointment authority to fill any jobs up through GS-11 or WG-11, and equivalent jobs under other federal pay systems. See "Veterans Readjustment Appointments under Veterans' Programs" in the Appendices.

APPLICATION FOR FEDERAL EMPLOYMENT: Standard Form 171, the application form used from 1968 through 1994 almost government-wide in the executive branch for federal hiring and promotion. It was abolished in 1995 as a *requirement* to apply for a federal job. Applicants who have paper copies or 171 software may continue to use it if they choose.

CAREER AMERICA CONNECTION: A telephone message system at (912) 757-3000. Callers get current, nationwide information on federal job openings and applications procedures, including customized messages from agencies. You may also request application materials. Have a pencil and paper handy if you call. You'll have to write down instructions on how to access the information.

CERTIFICATION: The process by which eligibles (qualified applicants) are ranked for appointment or promotion consideration.

CIVIL SERVICE REFORM ACT: The 1978 Act that revamped the federal civil service system, abolished the Civil Service Commission, created two independent agencies to assume its functions (the Office of Personnel Management and the Merit Systems Protection Board), and defined the merit principles that govern the civil service system. This Act provided for the most extensive revision since civil service was established in 1883.

CIVIL SERVICE SYSTEM: The federal government's competitive hiring system that fills all positions--whether new hires or promotions--on the merit of the applicants as measured against established standards or specific job requirements. Some agencies or personnel, however, are exempted. See **Competitive Service** below.

CLOSING DATE: The date by which an application and other requested application materials must be received by the agency that has announced a job vacancy. **Some agencies will accept applications that are postmarked by the closing date; others will not.** Sometimes a vacancy will be listed as "open" (meaning no set closing date), but this does not mean that you have unlimited time to get your application in. The application will be closed when the agency has found one or more likely candidates.

COMPETITIVE SERVICE: The federal personnel merit system governed by the Civil Service Reform Act of 1978 and administered by the Office of Personnel Management. The competitive service is based on principles of fair and equitable treatment in hiring and employment without regard to politics, race, color, religion, national origin, sex, marital status, age, or handicapping condition.

ELIGIBLE (used as a noun): An applicant rated as having met the qualifying standards for employment in a specific job or category of jobs.

EXAMINATION: This is one of the most widely misunderstood terms in the federal hiring process because most people think of an "examination" as a written "test." The "examination" is just the process by which an applicant's qualifications are measured against established standards for a category of jobs or the requirements of a specific job. The examination *may* be a written test resulting in a test score. In such case it is called an "assembled examination," meaning that applicants assemble at set times and places. Assembled examinations are rare for most occupations today.

For most jobs, the "examination" is the evaluation of the Optional Application Form 612, the resume, the SF-171, or whatever the applicant chooses to submit as an application. Subject matter experts or personnel officials examine the application. They rate applications for experience, education, training, skills, awards, and other factors. **Thus, when you complete your federal job application, you are in effect writing your own "test." Your application is actually a marketing piece to sell you and your skills.**

EXCEPTED POSITIONS: Federal jobs not covered by the competitive service, such as lawyers, chaplains, and Department of Veterans Affairs doctors, dentists, and nurses. Some overseas, maritime, and seasonal occupations are also excepted, as well as jobs in isolated locations. These positions are usually covered by a merit system administered by the agency. To apply, contact the agency.

Excepted positions also include about 2,000 patronage or political jobs at the highest level of government—positions held by policy makers and related staff who work closely with the President or his Cabinet. Such positions, often called "plum" jobs, are spread among the agencies. These political appointments include several hundred under secretaries and assistant secretaries who are appointed by the President with the advice and consent of the Senate.

Positions may be excepted from the competitive civil service by statute, by the President, or by the Office of Personnel Management. Excepted positions fall into the following categories:

Schedule A: Jobs that require no civil service examination and are not of a confidential or policy-making nature. Attorneys and others fall into this category.

Schedule B: Jobs that are not confidential or policy-making, but do require a non-competitive examination. Not many positions are filled under this schedule.

Schedule C: Key positions that require a close personal relationship with the head of the agency. The agency head is free to appoint persons of his or her choosing. These are also called political appointments.

Non-Career Senior Executive Service: Positions similar in nature to Schedule C jobs. Pay rates are negotiated from the pay system for executives. The agency head appoints people of his or her choice.

FACTOR EVALUATION SYSTEM: A position classification system that allows widely differing job categories to be evaluated in terms of their job elements and graded fairly. The idea is that all jobs have certain factors in common, such as the amount of knowledge required by the position, the nature of supervision required, the complexity of the work, the scope and effect of the responsibilities, the physical demands of the position, etc.

EXCEPTED SERVICE: Federal organizations and agencies whose personnel systems are not subject to the competitive service administered by the Office of Personnel Management. These exempted organizations include the Congress, the Judiciary, the Postal Service, and a number of agencies. These organizations and agencies fill their jobs through their own hiring systems. You will find a list of excepted agencies in the Appendices.

FEDERAL EMPLOYMENT INFORMATION CENTERS: (Also called Federal Job Information Centers.) Offices administered by the Office of Personnel Management that provide federal hiring information in 26 locations over the country. Many contain a Federal Job Information Touch Screen Computer to access worldwide federal job information. If you visit a center, you may wish to ask if a counselor is available.

FEDERAL JOB INFORMATION TOUCH SCREEN COMPUTER: User friendly, PC-based kiosk that provides job seekers with current federal job information by touching a computer screen. These kiosks are located in Federal Employment Information Centers, some federal personnel offices, and some state employment offices.

FEDERAL OCCUPATIONAL AND CAREER INFORMATION SYSTEM: A PC-based software program developed by the Office of Personnel Management to help job seekers find general information about federal careers and training opportunities. The career counseling software has an overview of 600 worldwide federal occupations, access to federal job opportunities, tips on completing application forms, a work interest test, and sample practice examinations. It is located in Federal Employment Information Centers, some federal personnel offices, and some state employment offices.

FEDERAL WAGE SYSTEM: The personnel and pay system for employees in trades, crafts, and labor occupations (blue collar workers). The pay rates are based on prevailing local rates for similar work in private industry.

FISCAL YEAR: The financial or budget year of the federal government. It begins on October 1 and ends on September 30 of the next year.

FREEZE: A situation in which all federal hiring stops until normal attrition reduces the number of employees to a predetermined level. A freeze can be declared government-wide or for certain departments or agencies. Often, certain categories of positions are excepted from a freeze. There are also "two for one" freezes, temporary freezes, selected occupation freezes, etc.

Don't let a federal job freeze stop you from job hunting. No freeze is airtight; there is always some federal hiring going on. Check carefully. The job you want may not be affected.

FULL TIME EQUIVALENT (FTE): A 40-hour job (or its equivalent, such as two 20-hour jobs). The Office of Management and Budget puts limits (ceilings) on how many FTEs an agency can have, depending on the agency's workload and budget.

GENERAL SCHEDULE: The uniform system of pay that applies to almost all federal white collar jobs and a few blue collar jobs. Under this system, positions are graded from GS-1 (least difficult work/lowest pay) to GS-18 (most difficult work/highest pay), regardless of the type of work.

By federal law passed in 1990, this uniform pay system is being phased out in favor of "locality pay" to bring federal salaries in line with private sector salaries in geographic areas where non-federal pay may be significantly higher. The law also abolished the supergrades (GS 16-18) and set up a new pay system for these positions, which are largely scientific and technical positions that have no supervisory or managerial responsibilities.

HANDBOOK X-118: A collection of qualifications standards that became obsolete in 1993. It contained written qualifications standards for white collar positions under the General Schedule. These standards described the experience and education required for every federal job at each grade level. This handbook was replaced by a shorter *Qualification Standards Handbook* that may be found in most personnel offices and in Federal Employment Information Centers.

LIST OF COLLEGE COURSES: The Office of Personnel Management Form 1170/17. The easiest way to complete this form is to fill in the top of the first page, sign and date the form on the appropriate page and staple a copy of your college transcript (or transcripts) in the middle. On the first page, under "Page 1," write "Please see attached transcript." However, if your education, especially graduate education, is critical to the occupation you're entering, or if it's the most qualifying experience you have for the job, fill out the entire form. Fill out the entire form as well if you can get credit under "Part III-Scholastic Achievement." Do not fill out form at all or send transcripts unless you are required to.

LOCALITY PAY: Special pay raises ranging from three to eight percent for federal workers in cities with a high cost of living such as Los Angeles, New York, and San Francisco. Congress set this tool in place to help achieve pay comparability between federal jobs and those in the private sector. The law (the Federal Employees Pay Comparability Act of 1990) calls not only for an annual raise for all employees on the General Schedule, but also a second adjustment based on locality. This gets complicated in practice. For example, in 1994, the nationwide adjustment was canceled, although employees in certain areas received raises.

MERIT PAY SYSTEM: An incentive pay system for federal supervisors and managers, GM 13-15. Instead of set increases, merit managers received pay increases that varied in amount according to the quality of their performance. The system, set by law on a trial basis for a few years, was abolished in 1994, and the salaries of merit managers are gradually being returned to the General Schedule.

MID-LEVEL POSITIONS: Jobs in grades 9-12 of the General Schedule. This term has gone out of use.

OCCUPATIONAL GROUP: A group of different positions that are related to each other or belong to the same field of work. The government classifies jobs into 22 occupational groups, such as Biological Sciences Group or Copyright, Patent and Trademark Group. A full listing of the groups and the various positions may be found in the *Handbook of Occupational Groups and Series of Classes*.

OFFICE OF PERSONNEL MANAGEMENT: The federal agency that regulates and administers the competitive service. Under the reinventing government initiative, the Office of Personnel Management is delegating many of its centralized personnel responsibilities directly to federal agencies. These responsibilities include recruiting, examining, training, and promoting people on the basis of their knowledge and skills (merit), regardless of their race, religion, sex, political influence, or other non-merit factors. The Office of Personnel Management is beginning to act less as a central personnel management authority and more as a consultant and advisor to federal agencies.

In general, the Office of Personnel Management's main obligation to you, the job seeker, is to provide information about jobs in the federal sector, not to take your application. There are exceptions to this rule, however, such as recruiting staff for positions that are hard to fill, like nurses in remote locations.

PANEL: A group of three subject matter experts who evaluate job applications (Optional Form 612, resume, or a SF-171) against the requirements of an announced position and develop a preliminary best qualified list.

PERFORMANCE APPRAISAL: A supervisor's evaluation of an employee's performance on the job based on established standards or a performance plan. Appraisals may be used as a basis for training, rewarding, reassigning, promoting, demoting (reducing-in-grade), retaining, and removing employees.

Many job announcements request a copy of an applicant's most recent performance appraisal. If you do not have a recent appraisal, ask your current or previous employer for one. You may even ask for a blank appraisal form from the federal agency from which you are seeking employment and have your current or previous employer complete it. Keep the original and make multiple copies to include with your application package.

POSITION CLASSIFICATION STANDARDS: Written standards that define the occupation and tell what is done in each position at each grade level in both General Schedule and wage grade jobs. This is a helpful tool that can be found in federal personnel offices and Federal Employment Information Centers.

QUALIFICATION STANDARDS HANDBOOK FOR GENERAL SCHEDULE POSITIONS: Issued by the Office of Personnel Management in 1993, this handbook describes the education and experience required for positions under the General Schedule. The short title is Qualification Standards Handbook.

REDUCTION-IN-FORCE (RIF): The firing or cutting back on the number of employees an agency has, usually because of budget cuts or a change in mission. This is a complex system in which employees are ranked on certain criteria such as length of government employment, grade, veterans status, and other factors. Those with the lowest ranks are demoted or dismissed until the authorized personnel ceiling is achieved.

Career and career-conditional employees who are RIFed are identified in priority order for reemployment to competitive positions in the commuting area where the separations occurred.

REGISTER: A list of eligibles (qualified job applicants) for a certain category of jobs.

REINSTATEMENT ELIGIBILITY: A condition in which a former competitive service employee may be rehired non-competitively.

SENIOR EXECUTIVE SERVICE (SES): A personnel and pay system for about 7,800 men and women who set policy and administer programs at the top levels of government. There are four types of SES appointments: career, non-career, limited term, and limited emergency.

SENIOR LEVEL POSITIONS: Jobs in grades 13-15 of the General Schedule. This term has gone out of use. For a time, employees with supervisory or managerial duties in this range were in the now-abolished merit pay system.

STANDARD FORM 15: Form used to claim 10-point veteran preference.

STATUS: Current employment in the competitive service or former civil service employment with reinstatement eligibility. Job announcements indicate whether a job is open to status or non-status candidates, but sometimes the words are not used. For example, if the area of consideration is "nationwide," non-status candidates may apply.

TELEPHONE APPLICATION PROCESSING SYSTEM (TAPS): A new system in which applicants can apply over the phone for federal employment. Currently, professional nurse and border patrol agents positions are operating under this system. Applicants are instructed to provide answers to questions by speaking or using the keys of a touch-tone telephone. The questions cover minimum qualifications, such as education and experience, citizenship, and job interest. OPM transcribes the responses and rates them on a computer within a day. Names of eligible applicants are immediately placed on a referral list and made available to federal agencies with jobs to fill. The number is (800) 800-8776.

VETERANS' PREFERENCE: The special hiring consideration given to qualified veterans. Federal job applications are rated numerically. Generally, five points are added for honorably discharged veterans. Ten points are added for disabled veterans and in some cases for their spouses, widows, widowers, or mothers. For example, if the weights and factors for a position add up to 100 points and an applicant with a 10-point veterans preference gets 80 points, another 10 points would be added to make a total competitive score of 90.

There are other preferences, too. Some positions may be reserved for veterans. On a register, qualified veterans may not be passed over in favor of a non-veteran. Ten-point veterans may also submit applications even if the register is closed.

WAGE GRADE WORKERS: Blue collar workers who are paid according to prevailing local rates.

Federal government attorney positions are in the excepted service and are not covered by the civil service procedures overseen by the Office of Personnel Management. To apply for a professional legal position that requires bar membership, contact the personnel office of the agency for which you wish to work and submit the application form or resume that the office requires. Generally, you will need a law school transcript. If the agency has a vacancy, it will contact you and arrange for a personal interview. (Note: Use your academic, professional, social and job-hunting networks to scout for information and contacts.)

If you are still in school, you should submit your application well in advance of the date you expect to graduate. If you're going to finish school in June, you should apply the preceding fall.

Bar Membership

All attorney positions require bar membership. In most cases, admission to the bar of any state or the District of Columbia is sufficient, regardless of where you'll be assigned.

Grade Levels Based on Education and Experience

Grade GS-9

The usual entry level job for attorneys in the government is GS-9. The GS-9 lawyer works under close supervision, and the job is considered a sort of legal internship. An LLB or JD degree is required.

Grade GS-11

Applicants may enter at a GS-11 level if they meet the GS-9 requirement and in addition have 1 year of professional experience, an LLM, or superior law student work or activities while earning the LLB or JD. These activities include:

✎   Academic standing in upper third of law school graduating class

✎   Work or achievement of significance on law school's official law review

✎   Special high-level honors for academic excellence such as election to the order of the Coif

✎   Winning a moot court competition or membership on the moot court team that represents the law school in competition with other law schools

✎   Full-time or continuous participation in a legal aid program or significant summer law office clerk experience or other equivalent evidence of clearly superior achievement, as determined by the hiring agency.

Grade GS-12

In unusual instances, a lawyer without previous experience may be hired at the GS-12, substituting education that is particularly relevant to the work of the hiring agency.

Higher Grade Levels

Agencies also hire more experienced lawyers at higher grades. These lawyers must have skills that the agencies need. Their grade levels correspond to their additional experience.

Some federal organizations are excepted from the competitive civil service overseen by the Office of Personnel Management. These organizations fill vacancies through their own competitive hiring systems and application forms or resumes. If you are interested in a job in these agencies, contact their personnel offices directly. The writing concepts and job hunting tips from this book apply to these organizations, although the forms and procedures may be different.

Under certain conditions, employees of agencies marked with an asterisk (*) may transfer to positions in the competitive civil service.

Phone numbers often change in the federal government. Please check the blue pages in the telephone directory for current numbers if those listed are non-working numbers.

Central Intelligence Agency
Washington, DC 20505
Personnel: (703) 482-0677
Vacancies: (800) 562-7242

Defense Intelligence Agency
Civilian Personnel Division
Pentagon
Washington, DC 20301

Executive Protective Service
(Secret Service Uniformed Branch)
1800 G Street, NW
Washington, DC 20223

Federal Bureau of Investigation
Personnel Office
Room 6050, J. Edgar Hoover Bldg.
Washington, DC 20535
Personnel: (202) 324-4981
Vacancies: (202) 324-3674

Federal Reserve System
Board of Governors
20th St. and Constitution Ave., NW
Washington, DC 20551

General Accounting Office *
Personnel Office
441 G Street, NW
Washington, DC 20548
Personnel: (202) 512-6092

National Science Foundation
1800 G Street NW, Rm 208
Washington, DC 20550
Personnel   (202) 357-7602
Vacancies   (703) 306-0080
(Only scientific, engineering, and a small number of high-level managerial positions are excepted. Administrative positions are predominantly in the competitive service.)

National Security Agency
Fort Meade, MD 20775

Nuclear Regulatory Commission *
Division of Organization of Personnel
Recruitment Branch
Washington, DC 20555

Postal Rate Commission *
Administrative Office
Room 500, 2000 L St., NW
Washington, DC 20268

US Postal Service
475 L'Enfant Plaza, SW
Washington, DC 20260
Corporate Personnel: (202) 286-3646
(Also contact your local postmaster.)

US Department of State *
Employment Information Office
Room 2819, 22nd and D St., NW
Washington, DC 20547
Job Hot Line (202) 647-7284
* Skilled specialists and experienced secretaries in the State Department are the only employees who may be able to transfer to competitive civil service; all others must apply to take the foreign service exam.

Tennessee Valley Authority *
Human Resource Services
400 West Summit Hill Drive
Knoxville, TN 37902-1499
(615) 632-3341

United States Mission to the United Nations*
799 United Nations Plaza
New York, NY 10017

Department of Veterans Affairs *
810 Vermont Ave., NW
Washington, DC 20420
Personnel   (202) 523-8687
TDD   (202) 233-3225
Inquire about employment opportunities in VA Medical Centers nationwide. Vacancies exist for doctors, nurses, and a variety of medical positions.

Judicial Branch of the Government (except the Administrative Office of the United States Courts and the United States Customs Courts)

Legislative Branch of the Government (includes Senators' offices, Representatives' offices, the Library of Congress, and the Capitol, but not the Government Printing Office.)

Appendix C
Federal Employment
Information Centers

Touch Screen Service Is Available in Each Center.

Alabama: Huntsville
520 Wynn Dr., NW., 35816-3426
(205) 837-0894
Telephone Service: M-F/9-1
Staff on Duty: M-F/8-1
Self Service: M-F/1-4

Alaska: Anchorage
222 West 7th Avenue, #22, Rm 156, 99513-7572
(907) 271-5821
Staff on Duty: T-Th/11-1

Arizona: Phoenix
Century Plaza Bldg, #1415,
3225 North Central Avenue, 85012
(602) 640-4800
Self Service: M-F/8-4:30

Arkansas: (See San Antonio, TX)

California: Los Angeles
9650 Flair Drive, #100A,
El Monte, 91731
(818) 575-6510
Staff on Duty: M-F/9-3

Sacramento
1029 J Street, #202, 95814
(916) 551-1464
Staff on Duty: M-F/9-12

San Diego
Federal Bldg, #4218,
880 Front Street, 92101
(619) 557-6165

Staff on Duty: M-F/9-12
Self Service: M-F/8-9; 12-3

San Francisco
211 Main Street, 2nd Floor, #235
(mail) PO Box 7405, 94120
Staff on Duty: M-F/9-12

Colorado: Denver
12345 West Alameda Pkwy, Lakewood
(mail) PO Box 25167, 80225
(303) 969-7050
For forms, call (303) 969-7055
Staff on Duty: M-F/12-3:45
Self Service: M-F/9-12

Connecticut: Hartford
Federal Bldg, #133,
450 Main Street, 06103
(For additional information services, see
Massachusetts)

Delaware: (See Philadelphia, PA)

District of Columbia:
Washington, DC Metropolitan Area
1900 E Street NW, #1416, 20415
(202) 606-2700 (Staff on Duty: M-F/8-4)

Florida: Miami
Claude Pepper Federal Bldg, #1222,
51 SW First Avenue, 33130
(305) 536-6738
Staff on Duty: M-F/9-4
Orlando

Commodore Bldg, #125,
3444 McCrory Place, 32803
(407) 648-6148 (Staff on Duty: M-F/9-4)

Georgia: Atlanta
Richard B. Russell Federal Bldg, #940A,
75 Spring St. SW, 30303
(404) 331-4315
Staff on Duty: M-F/9-1
Self Service: M-F/8-4

Hawaii: Honolulu
(and other Hawaiian Islands and Pacific overseas)
Federal Bldg, #5316,
300 AlaMoana Blvd., 96850
(808) 541-2791
Staff on Duty: M-F/9-12

Idaho: (See Washington State)

Illinois: Chicago
175 W. Jackson Blvd., #530, 60604
(312) 353-6192
Self Service: M-F/7-4:45
(For Madison and St. Clair Counties, see St. Louis, MO listing)

Indiana: Indianapolis
Minton-Capehart Federal Bldg., #368,
575 N. Pennsylvania St., 46204
(313) 226-6950
(For additional information services in the State of Indiana, see Michigan. For Clark, Dearborn and Floyd Counties, see Ohio listing)

Iowa: (See Kansas City, Missouri)
(816) 426-7757
(For Scott County, see Illinois)

Kansas: (See Kansas City, Missouri)
(816) 426-7820

Kentucky: (See Ohio listing)
(For Henderson County, see Michigan)

Louisiana: New Orleans

1515 Poydras St., #608, 70112
(504) 589-2764/ 24-Hour Jobline
Self Service: M-F/8-5

Maine: (See Massachusetts)

Maryland: Baltimore
Marsh and McLennan Bldg,
300 West Pratt St., 21201
(Self Service only, M-F/9-4. For mail or telephone, see Philadelphia, PA)

Massachusetts: Boston
Thos. P. O'Neill, Jr., Federal Bldg,
10 Causeway St., 02222
(617) 565-5900
24-Hour Job Info: Daily (617) 565-5900
Staff on Duty: M-F/9-2
Self Service: M-F/6-6

Michigan: Detroit
477 Michigan Avenue, #565, 48226
(313) 226-6950
Self Service: M-F/8-4:30

Minnesota: Twin Cities
Bishop Henry Whipple Federal Bldg,
1 Federal Dr., #501, Ft. Snelling, Twin Cities 55111
(612) 725-3430
Self Service: M-F/7:30-4:30

Mississippi: (See Alabama)

Missouri: Kansas City
Federal Bldg, #134,
601 E. 12th St., 64106
(816) 426-5702
Self Service: M-F/8-4
(For Counties west of and including Mercer, Grundy, Livingston, Carroll, Saline, Pettis, Benton, Hickory, Dallas, Webster, Douglas, and Ozark)

St. Louis
400 Old Post Office Bldg,
815 Olive St., 63101
(314) 539-2285

Self Service: M-F/8-4
(For all other Missouri Counties not listed
under Kansas City above)

Montana: (See Colorado)
(303) 969-7050

Nebraska: (See Kansas City, Missouri)
(816) 426-7816

Nevada: (For Clark, Lincoln and Nye
Counties, see Los Angeles, CA; for all other
Nevada Counties not listed above, see
Sacramento, CA)

New Hampshire: Portsmouth
Thomas McIntyre Federal Bldg, 1st Floor
Lobby, 80 Daniel Street, 03801
(For additional information services, see
Massachusetts)

New Jersey: Newark
Rodino Federal Bldg, 2nd Floor,
970 Broad St., 07102
(For additional information services in Bergen,
Essex, Hudson, Hunterdon, Middlesex, Morris,
Passaic, Somerset, Sussex, Union, and Warren
Counties, see New York City, NY. For
additional information services in Atlantic,
Burlington, Camden, Cape May, Cumberland,
Gloucester, Mercer, Monmouth, Ocean, and
Salem Counties, see Philadelphia, PA)

New Mexico: Albuquerque
505 Marquette Avenue, #910, 87102
(505) 766-2906
Staff on Duty: M-F/8-5

New York: New York City
Jacob K. Javits Federal Bldg, 2nd Floor, #120,
26 Federal Plaza, 10278
(212) 264-0422/0423
Staff on Duty: M-F/10-12
Self Service: M-F/8-5

Syracuse:
P. O. Box 7257,
100 S. Clinton St., 13261

(315) 423-5660
Self Service: M-F/9-4

North Carolina: Raleigh
4407 Bland Rd., #202, 27609
(919) 790-2822
Staff on Duty: M-F/8-4:30
Self Service: M-F/8-4:30

North Dakota: (See Minnesota)

Ohio: Dayton
Federal Bldg, #506,
200 West Second St., 45402
(513) 225-2720
Self Service: M-F/7-6
(For Van Wert, Auglaize, Hardin, Marion,
Crawford, Richland, Ashland, Wayne, Stark,
Carroll, Columbiana Counties and farther
north, see Michigan)

Oklahoma: (See San Antonio, TX)

Oregon: Portland
Federal Bldg, #376,
1220 SW 3rd Avenue, 97204
(503) 326-3141
Staff on Duty: M-F/12-3
Self Service: M-F/8-12

Pennsylvania: Harrisburg
Federal Bldg, #168,
P. O. Box 761, 17108
(717) 782-4494
Staff on Duty: MTTh8-12

Philadelphia
Wm. J. Green, Jr., Federal Bldg,
600 Arch St., 19106
(215) 597-7440
Staff on Duty: M-F/10:30-2:30
Self Service: M-F/8:30-3:30

Pittsburgh
Federal Bldg, #119,
1000 Liberty Avenue, 15222
(Walk-in only. For mail or telephone, see
Philadelphia listing)

Self Service: M-F/9-4

Puerto Rico: San Juan
US Federal Bldg, #328,
150 Carlos Chardon Avenue, 00918
Staff on Duty: M-F/9-12:30
Self Service: M-F/7:30-9; 12:30-4
24-Hour Job Info: M-F only at (809) 766-5242

Rhode Island: (See Massachusetts)

South Carolina: (See Raleigh, NC)

South Dakota: (See Minnesota)

Tennessee: Memphis
200 Jefferson Avenue, #1312
Self Service: M-F/8-4
(Walk-in only. For mail or telephone, see
Alabama listing)

Texas: Corpus Christi
(See San Antonio)
(512) 884-8113

Dallas
1100 Commerce St., #6B10, 75242
(214) 767-8035
Self Service: M-F/8-5

Harlingen (See San Antonio)
(512) 412-0722

Houston (See San Antonio)
(713) 759-0455

San Antonio
8610 Broadway, #305, 78217
(210) 805-2423
For forms, call (210) 805-2406
Staff on Duty: M-F/8-5
24-Hour Job Info: (210) 805-2402

Utah: (See Colorado)

Vermont: Burlington
Federal Bldg, 1st Floor Lobby,

11 Elmwood Avenue, 05401
(For additional information services, see
Massachusetts)

Virgin Islands: (See Puerto Rico)
(809) 774-8790

Virginia: Norfolk
For mail only:
Federal Bldg, #500,
200 Granby St., 23510
(804) 441-3355
Telephone Service: M-F/8-4

For walk-in only:
National Guard Armory, #18A,
3777 E. Virginia Beach Blvd.
Staff on Duty: M-F/8:30-4:30

Washington: Seattle
Federal Bldg, #110,
915 Second Avenue, 98174
(206) 220-6400
Staff on Duty: M-F/12-3:30
Self Service: M-F/8-12

Washington, DC:
(See District of Columbia)

West Virginia: (See Ohio)
(513) 225-2866

Wisconsin:
(For Dane, Grant, Green, Iowa, Lafayette,
Rock, Jefferson, Walworth, Milwaukee,
Waukesha, Racine, and Kenosha Counties, see
Illinois listing,(312) 353-6189. For all other
Wisconsin Counties not listed above, see
Minnesota listing, (612) 725-3430)

Wyoming: (See Colorado)

The following is a partial list of the personnel offices of the departments and agencies in the Washington, DC area. Government phone numbers often change. If the number listed is not correct, or to get other personnel office listings, please refer to the blue pages of the DC, northern Virginia, and suburban Maryland telephone directories. Address inquires to "Personnel Office," if it is not indicated in the address below.

Agriculture

Department of Agriculture
Office of Personnel, Rm SM-7
AG PROMENADE
12th & Independence Ave. SW
Washington, DC 20250-9650
Personnel   202-720-5626

Agriculture Research Service
Personnel Division
6305 Ivy Lane, Rm 106
Greenbelt, MD 20770-1435
Personnel   301-344-1518
Vacancies   301-344-1124
                      301-344-2288

Farmers Home Administration
Human Resources Division
501 School Street, 3rd Floor .
Washington, DC 20024
Personnel   202-245-5561

Forest & Nutrition Service
301 Park Center Drive, Rm 620
Alexandria, VA 22302
Personnel   703-756-3351

Forest Service
Personnel Management Staff
Rosslyn Plaza East, Rm 913
Rosslyn, VA 22209
Personnel   703-235-8145
Vacancies   703-235-2730

Soil Conservation Service
Personnel Staff, Rm 5209-S
14th & Independence Avenue SW
Washington, DC 20013
Personnel   202-720-4264
Vacancies   202-720-6365

Commerce

Office of the Secretary
Department of Commerce
14th & Constitution Ave. NW, Rm 5001
Washington, DC 20230
Personnel   202-482-2560
Vacancies   202-482-5138
                      202-482-1533
TDD   202-482-0325

Bureau of the Census
Personnel Division
Rm 1412 FOB #3

Washington, DC 20233

Personnel	301-763-7470
Vacancies	301-763-6064
TDD	301-763-4944

International Trade Administration

14th & Constitution Ave. NW, Rm 4809
Washington, DC 20230

| Personnel | 202-482-5138 |

National Institute of Standards & Technology

Administration Bldg, Rm A123
Gaithersburg, MD 20899

Personnel	301-975-3007
Vacancies	301-926-4851
TDD	301-975-2039

National Oceanic & Atmospheric Administration

Career Resource Center
1335 East-West Highway, Rm 2262
Silver Spring, MD 20910

| Personnel | 301-713-0677 |

Office of Inspector General

Attn: James D. Back, Rm 7713
14th & Constitution Avenue NW
Washington, DC 20230

Personnel	202-377-4948
Vacancies	202-377-3476
TDD	202-377-5897

Patent and Trademark Office

Office of Personnel
2011 Crystal Drive
Arlington, VA 22202

Personnel	703-305-8231
Vacancies	703-305-4221
TDD	703-305-8586

Defense

Defense Logistics Agency

Staff Director
Civilian Personnel
Cameron Station

Alexandria, VA 22304-6100

| Personnel | 703-274-7088 |
| Vacancies | 703-274-7372 |

Defense Mapping Agency

8613 Lee Highway
Fairfax, VA 22031-2137

| Personnel | 703-285-9148 |
| Vacancies | 703-285-9461 |

Defense Uniformed Services University of Health and Sciences

Civilian Personnel
Bethesda, MD 20814

| Vacancies | 703-875-7490 |
| TDD | 703-516-0025 |

Department of the Air Force

NCR-SPTGDPC, CPO 1100
The Pentagon, Rm 5E871
Washington, DC 20330

| Personnel | 703-695-4389 |
| Vacancies | 703-693-6550 |

Andrews Air Force Base

Bldg 1535, Rm E212
89th MSSQ
Andrews AFB, MD 20331-5964

| Personnel | 301-981-5431 |

Bolling Air Force Base

Civilian Personnel
Bldg P-20, Rm 240
1100 RMG/DPC
Washington, DC 20333

| Personnel | 202-767-5449 |

Department of the Army

Hoffman Civilian Personnel Office
Hoffman Bldg II, Rm 1S39
200 Stovall Street
Attn: ANCP-HPR
Alexandria, VA 22332-0800

| Personnel | 703-325-8840 |
| Vacancies | 703-325-8841 |

Vacancies List   202-514-6818
TDD   202-514-7972

Bureau of Prisons
HOLC Bldg, Rm 161
Washington, DC 20543
Personnel   202-307-1304
Vacancies   202-514-6388

Drug Enforcement Administration
700 Army-Navy Drive
Arlington, VA 22202
Personnel   202-307-4055
Vacancies   202-307-5550
TDD   202-307-8903

Federal Bureau of Investigation
Personnel Office
JEH Bldg, Rm 6050
10th Street & Pennsylvania Avenue NW
Washington, DC 20535
Personnel   202-324-4981
Vacancies   202-324-3674

Immigration & Naturalization Service
Personnel & Training
CAB Bldg, Rm 6023
425 I Street NW
Washington, DC 20536
Personnel   202-514-2530
Vacancies   202-514-4301

US Marshal Service
Personnel Office, Suite 890
600 Army-Navy Drive
Arlington, VA 22202
Personnel   202-307-9433
Vacancies   202-307-9400/9600

State Department

Foreign Service
Recruitment Division
PO Box 9317
Arlington, VA 22219
Vacancies   703-875-7490
TDD   703-812-2264

State Department
Civil Service
Employment Information Office
22nd & D Street NW, Rm 2819
Washington, DC 20520
Personnel   202-647-7284
TDD   202-647-7256

Transportation

Department of Transportation
Central Employment Information M-18.1
400 7th Street SW, Rm 9113
Washington, DC 20590
Personnel   202-366-9394
Vacancies   202-366-9397
TDD   202-366-9402

Federal Aviation Administration
800 Independence Avenue SW
Washington, DC 20591
Personnel   202-267-3870
Vacancies   202-267-3902/8007

Urban Mass Transportation Administration
400 7th Street SW, Rm 7101
Washington, DC 20590
Personnel   202-366-2513
Vacancies   202-366-5525

Treasury

Department of Treasury
Director of Personnel, Rm 4151
Employment & Executive Services
Pennsylvania Avenue & Madison Place NW
Washington, DC 20220
Personnel   202-377-1460
Vacancies   202-377-1029

Internal Revenue Service
111 Constitution Avenue NW, Rm 1034
Washington, DC 20224
Personnel   202-622-6340
Vacancies   202-622-6340

US Customs Service
2120 L Street NW, 6th Floor
Washington, DC 20037
Personnel   202-634-5270
TDD   202-634-2069

Veterans Affairs

Veterans Affairs
810 Vermont Avenue NW
Washington, DC 20420
Personnel   202-523-8687
TDD   202-233-3225

Veterans Affairs Medical Center
50 Irving Street NW, 05-A
Washington, DC 20422
Personnel   202-745-8204
Vacancies   202-745-8200

Independent Agencies

Action
Personnel Management Division
1100 Vermont Avenue NW, Rm 1151
Washington, DC 20525
Personnel   202-606-5263
Vacancies   202-606-5000

Agency for International Development
2401 E Street NW, Rm 1127
Washington, DC 20523
Personnel   202-663-1512

Central Intelligence Agency
Office of Personnel
Washington, DC 20505
Personnel   703-482-0677 or
                   800-562-7242

Commodity Futures Trading Commission
2033 K Street NW, Rm 202
Washington, DC 20581
Personnel   202-254-3275
Vacancies   202-254-3346

Environmental Protection Agency
401 M Street SW
Washington, DC 20460
Personnel   202-260-2090
Vacancies   202-260-5055

Equal Employment Opportunity Commission
1801 L Street NW
Washington, DC 20507
Personnel   202-663-4900
TDD   202-663-7025

Export-Import Bank of the US
Lafayette Bldg, Rm 1005
811 Vermont Avenue NW
Washington, DC 20571
Personnel   202-565-3300

Federal Communications Commission
1919 M Street NW, Rm 216
Washington, DC 20554
Personnel   202-418-0126
TDD   202-632-6999

Federal Deposit Insurance Corporation
Washington, DC 20929-9990
Personnel   202-942-3540

Federal Emergency Management Agency
500 C Street SW, Rm 816
Washington, DC 20472
Vacancies   202-646-3244

Federal Energy Regulatory Commission
Washington, DC 20426
Personnel   202-357-0992
Vacancies   202-219-2791

Federal Labor Relations Authority
500 C Street SW, 2nd Floor
Washington, DC 20424
Personnel   202-482-6660

Federal Trade Commission
Pennsylvania Avenue & 6th Street NW
Washington, DC 20580
Personnel   202-326-2022

Vacancies   202-326-2020
TDD   202-326-2502

General Accounting Office
Recruitment Office, Rm 4043
441 G Street NW
Washington, DC 20548
Personnel   202-512-6092

General Services Administration
18th & F Streets NW
Washington, DC 20405
Personnel   202-501-0370
Vacancies   202-273-3524

General Services Administration
National Capital Region
7th & D Streets SW
Washington, DC 20407
Personnel   202-708-5300
Vacancies   202-273-3577
TDD   202-708-5300

Federal Information Relay Service
800-877-8339

Government Printing Office
Employment Branch 6, Rm C106
North Capital & H Streets NW
Washington, DC 20401
Personnel   202-512-1198

International Trade Commission
500 E Street SW, Rm 314-B
Washington, DC 20436
Personnel   202-205-2651

Interstate Commerce Commission
12th & Constitution Avenue NW
Washington, DC 20423
Personnel   202-482-3765
Vacancies   202-482-5138

Merit Systems Protection Board
1120 Vermont Avenue NW, Rm 850
Washington, DC 20419
Personnel   202-653-5916
Vacancies   202-254-8013

TDD   202-653-8896

NASA
300 E Street SW
Washington, DC 20546
Personnel   202-358-1560

NASA Goddard Space Flight Center
Bldg 1, Rm 160
Greenbelt, MD 20771
Personnel   301-286-7918
Vacancies   301-286-5326

National Archives & Records Administration
7th & Pennsylvania Avenue NW, Rm 9108
Washington, DC 20408
Personnel   301-713-6760

National Endowment for the Arts
1100 Pennsylvania Avenue NW, Rm 208
Washington, DC 20506
Personnel   202-682-5405
Vacancies   202-682-5799

National Endowment for the Humanities
1100 Pennsylvania Avenue NW, Rm 417
Washington, DC 20506
Personnel   202-606-8415
Vacancies   202-606-8281

National Gallery of Art
Personnel Office
Washington, DC 20565
Personnel   202-842-6298
TDD   202-789-3021

National Labor Relations Board
1717 Pennsylvania Avenue NW, Rm 334
Washington, DC 20570
Personnel   202-273-3900
TDD   202-634-1669

National Library of Medicine
Bldg 38, Rm 2N05
8600 Rockville Pike
Bethesda, MD 20896

Personnel	301-496-4943
Vacancies	301-496-2403
TDD	301-496-9452

National Science Foundation
1800 G Street NW, Rm 208
Washington, DC 20550

| Personnel | 202-357-7602 |
| Vacancies | 703-306-0080 |

Office of Management & Budget
Personnel Management Division
725 17th Street NW, Rm 4013
Washington, DC 20503

| Personnel | 202-395-3765 |
| Vacancies | 202-395-5892 |

Office of Personnel Management
1900 E Street NW, Rm 1447
Washington, DC 20415

| Personnel | 202-606-2424 |
| TDD | 202-606-2118 |

Peace Corps
1990 K Street NW, Rm 7600
Washington, DC 20526

Personnel	202-606-3400
Vacancies	202-606-3214 or
	800-424-8580 ext 2214

Securities & Exchange Commission
450 Fifth Street NW, Rm C-145
Washington, DC 20549

| Personnel | 202-942-4150 |

Small Business Administration
409 Third St., SW, Suite 4200
Washington, DC 20416

| Personnel | 202-205-6780 |

Smithsonian Institution
955 L'Enfant Plaza, Suite 2100
Washington, DC 20560

| Personnel | 202-287-3100 |
| Vacancies | 202-287-3102 |

Social Security Administration
Rm G-120 West High Rise Bldg
6401 Security Boulevard
Baltimore, MD 21235

| Personnel | 410-965-4506 |
| TDD | 410-965-4404 |

US Information Agency
301 4th Street SW, Rm 518
Washington, DC 20547

| Personnel | 202-619-4659 |
| Vacancies | 202-619-4539 |

US Postal Service
Personnel Division, Rm 1813
475 L'Enfant Plaza West SW
Washington, DC 20260

| Personnel | 202-268-3646 |
| Vacancies | 800-562-8777 |

US Soldiers and Airmens Home
Rock Creek Church Road at Upshur Street
NW
Washington, DC 20317

| Personnel | 202-722-3215 |
| Vacancies | 202-722-3206 |

Voice of America
330 Independence Avenue SW, Rm 1543
Washington, DC 20547

| Personnel | 202-619-3117 |
| Vacancies | 202-619-0909 |

Sample Agency Announcement

United States Department of Agriculture
VACANCY ANNOUNCEMENT

Candidates will be considered without discrimination for any non-merit reason such as race, color, religion, sex, national origin, age, marital status, physical or mental handicap, or membership or nonmembership in an employee organization.

POSITION TITLE, SERIES & GRADE:
Executive Director, GS-301-14
(Excepted Service)

ANNOUNCEMENT NO: 95-RO1
OPENING DATE: January 1, 1995
CLOSING DATE: February 11, 1995

PROMOTION POTENTIAL: GS-15

POSITION LOCATION:
USDA
Rural Business & Cooperative
Development Service
CT State Rural Development Council
Winsted, CT

SEND COMPLETED APPLICATION
TO:
Human Resources,
USDA, Farmers Home Administration
14th & Independence Ave., S.W.
Washington, D.C. 20250-0700
Leslie Carlson (202) 382-0307

For copies of the announcement,
Please call the Job Hotline at
(202) 245 - 5606

Applications may be taken to
Room 4031S

* Completed Application Package must be post-marked in the Washington, DC office by the closing date.

AREA OF CONSIDERATION: ALL SOURCES (All Federal and nonfederal applicants are eligible to apply.)

EXCEPTED SERVICE: Appointment to this position will be under a Schedule B Hiring Authority. This appointment does not confer competitive status in the Federal Service; however, the employee will be eligible for Federal Employment benefits. Appointment and termination are joint decisions between the office of the Presidential Initiative and the State Rural Development Council.

RELOCATION: Relocation expenses will NOT be paid by the Federal Government. All expenses for Relocation must be borne by the appointee.

POSITION: The incumbent serves as Executive Director to the Connecticut State Rural Development Council. As such, provides administrative, technical and management support to the Council on a wide variety of rural development issues. Exercises disbursement authority regarding the Council's budget. Coordinates Council efforts with other agencies of Federal, State and/or local governments.

BASIC ELIGIBILITY REQUIREMENTS: Applicants must show one year of specialized experience which is in or directly related to the position. The applicant's work experience must clearly provide evidence of broad expert knowledge and application of rural development, economic development, and/or community development practices and principles. This experience must have been equivalent to the next lower grade level to the position for which you are applying. Experience must include extensive and in-depth responsibilities for developing broad-based, complex community plans; development of high level resources, facilities or services covering multiple areas required by communities; extensive work on attracting new and varied industries to low income or economically depressed areas; or development of comprehensive social or economic development strategies impacting broad areas.

For supervisory or managerial positions, candidate is subject to a probationary period unless prior supervisory or managerial experience is credible.

THE USE OF POSTAGE-PAID AGENCY ENVELOPES IN FILING APPLICATIONS IS A VIOLATION OF FEDERAL LAW.

EVALUATION CRITERIA: (Read Application Procedures Below Carefully)

1.   KNOWLEDGE OF FEDERAL AND STATE PRACTICES, PROCEDURES, LAWS AND REGULATIONS PERTAINING TO RURAL SOCIOECONOMIC AND COMMUNITY DEVELOPMENT ISSUES.

2   SKILL AND ACHIEVEMENT IN MANAGING OR LEADING RURAL PROJECTS. (OR PROGRAMS DIRECTLY RELATED TO RURAL DEVELOPMENT ISSUES) AND MAINTAINING EFFECTIVE WORKING RELATIONSHIPS AT ALL LEVELS.

3.   SKILL IN ATTAINING ORGANIZATIONAL GOALS BY MOTIVATING AND LEADING AN ORGANIZATION CONSISTING OF INDIVIDUALS REPRESENTING DIVERSE INTERESTS.

4.   ABILITY TO COMMUNICATE E.G.: ORALLY AND WRITTEN; TO DIVERSE GROUPS OR INDIVIDUALS. EXPERIENCE IN PUBLIC SPEAKING, AND/OR CONDUCTING MEETINGS/CONFERENCES.

5.   ABILITY TO MAKE EFFECTIVE USE OF RESEARCH-BASED KNOWLEDGE ABOUT RURAL CONDITIONS AND TRENDS, AND THE EFFECTIVENESS OF RURAL DEVELOPMENT PROGRAMS AND STRATEGIES.

APPLICATION PACKAGE: Those desiring consideration MUST submit the following forms:

1.   Application for Federal Employment Form, SF-171 (Rev. 6-88), or optional Application for Federal Employment, OP-612, or a resume. Only one of these must be submitted in the application package;

2.   Evaluation Criteria - all applicants MUST list each evaluation criteria separately and specifically address each; including specific tasks, assignments, problems resolved, and results achieved. RESPONSES FOR ANY ONE EVALUATION CRITERIA SHOULD NOT NORMALLY EXCEED TWO PAGES;

3.   Performance Evaluation

   A.   Federal employees must submit the most recent Performance Appraisal (within the last 18 months).

   B.   Non-Federal Candidates MUST submit 2 letters of recommendation that clearly address their candidate's ability to perform the duties of the position.

SUBMISSION OF ALL REQUESTED DOCUMENTS ABOVE IS MANDATORY. FAILURE TO SUBMIT ANY OF THE ABOVE REQUESTED DOCUMENTS WILL ELIMINATE THE APPLICANTS FROM CONSIDERATION FOR THIS POSITION.

Applicants are also requested, BUT NOT REQUIRED, to submit Form AD-1007, Background Survey Questionnaire. This form requests information that is used for statistical purposes only. This form is strictly voluntary and the information it contains is not provided to the selecting official nor is it maintained as a permanent part of the promotion file. Vacancy packages submitted will not be returned to applicants.

SAMPLE OPM ANNOUNCEMENT

U.S. OFFICE OF PERSONNEL MANAGEMENT
OFFICE OF WASHINGTON EXAMINING SERVICES
1900 E STREET, NW
WASHINGTON, DC 20415

COMPETITIVE VACANCY ANNOUNCEMENT

Position: Auditor, GS-511-7

STARTING SALARY: GS-7 = $26,259

ANNOUNCEMENT NO: WA-BE-5-0581DM   FJOL CONTROL NUMBER: WA6725

OPENING DATE: 01/17/95 CLOSING DATE: 01/31/95 PROMOTION POTENTIAL: Promotion potential exists to the GS-12 grade level.

DUTY LOCATION: U.S. DEPARTMENT OF THE NAVY
NAVY COMPTROLLER PROGRAM
MANAGEMENT OFFICE
ARLINGTON, VA

AREA OF CONSIDERATION: ALL SOURCES   **Number of Vacancies:** 6

CONTACT PHONE NUMBER:

Call (202) 606-2700. When the recorded message begins please listen and follow the instructions until you are asked "if you already know the message number you would like to hear enter number 2, you may enter 901 at this point to request an application package (be sure to specify announcement number.) You may also select message code 900 for information about additional vacancies.

MAJOR DUTIES:

The incumbent will be a member of an audit team performing a variety of assignments in conducting financial and operational audits. Receives intensive on-the-job and classroom training in planning, gathering information through interviews with activity personnel, and reporting an audit. Examines accounting documents and summary records to determine proper application of regulatory requirements. Consolidates information pertinent to the audit of records using prescribed format. Reviews functional program manuals to gain knowledge of audit subjects under evaluation. Attends pre-audit and exit conferences to learn presentation techniques. Demonstrates increasing ability to use communication skills, written and oral, in all phrases of auditing. Follows detailed instructions as to the techniques and practices of accounting, management, and auditing.

QUALIFICATION REQUIREMENTS: All applicants must meet the basic requirements outlined below:

A. A degree in accounting or a degree in a related field such as business administration, finance, or public administration that includes or was supplemented by 24 semester hours in accounting. The 24 semester hours may include up to 6 hours credit in business law.

OR

B. Combination of education and experience - A least 4 years of experience in accounting, or an equivalent combination of accounting experience, college level education, and training that provided professional accounting knowledge. Applicant's background must also include at least one of the following:

1. 24 semester hours in accounting or auditing courses (up to 6 hours may be in business law) of appropriate type and quality.

2. A certificate as Certified Public Accountant or a Certified Internal Auditor, obtained through written examination.

3. Completion of the requirements for a degree that included substantial course work in accounting or auditing, e.g., 15 semester hours, but that does not fully satisfy the 24-semester-hour requirement of paragraph A, provided that (a) the applicant has successfully demonstrated the ability to perform work of the GS-11 or higher grade level in accounting, auditing, or a related field, e.g.,.valuation engineering or financial institution examining; (b) a panel of at least two higher level professional accountants or auditors has determined that the applicant has demonstrated a good knowledge of accounting and of related and underlying fields that equals in breadth, depth, currency, and level of advancement that which is normally associated with successful completion of the 4-year course of study described in paragraph A: and except for literal nonconformance to the requirement of 24 semester hours in accounting, the applicant's education, training, and experience fully meet the specified requirements.

Crediting Accounting Technician Experience:

Applicants who qualify through a combination of college education and work experience and who meet the 24 semester-hour accounting course work requirement may use experience gained in an accounting technician position to meet the 4 year experience requirement. Qualifying accounting technician experience includes at least one year at the GS-5 or higher level and demonstrates the potential for competent performance in a variety of types of professional accounting and auditing positions.

Professional Accounting Knowledge:

Persons who do not possess the required minimum education will be evaluated on their professional accounting knowledge gained in a variety of increasingly difficult work assignments and on any applicable training or course work completed. Claimed evidence of experience must demonstrate full performance level work in accounting/auditing work (or a directly related field, e.g., valuation engineering or financial institution examining) comparable to at least the GS-11 level and demonstrate a good knowledge of the specialty field and the related and underlying discipline comparable to at least a bachelor's degree.

FOR THE GS-7 GRADE POSITION:

In addition to meeting the basic requirements as described above applicants must meet one of the following requirements:

A. One full year of graduate level education, or a master's degree, LL.B., J.D., LL.M., PH.D.

OR

B. Completion of all the requirements of a bachelor's degree and meet the following under Superior Academic Achievement provision: S.A.A is based on (1) class standing (2) grade-point average (3) honor society membership:

    1.   Class standing: Upper third of the graduating class in the college or university.

    2.   A grade-point average of "B" (a GPA of 2.95 or higher) for all completed undergraduate courses, or those completed in the last 2 years of undergraduate study.

    3.   A grade-point average of "B+" (a GPA of 3.45 or higher) for all courses in your major field of study, or those courses in your major completed in the last two years of undergraduate study.

    4.   Honor Society membership: Membership in one of the national scholastic honor societies listed in the Association of College Honor Societies: Booklet of Information (1992-95) and Bairdard's Manual of American College Fraternities (1991).

Note: If more than 10 percent of your undergraduate course work (credit hours) was taken on a pass/fail or similar basis, your claim must be based on class standing or membership in an honor society.

OR

C. One year of experience equivalent to at least the GS-5 grade level as described below:

A professional knowledge of the concepts and principles of accounting needed to perform assignments designed to (1) provide experience in the practical application of accounting concepts, principles, procedures, and techniques; (2) develop familiarity with the accounting systems, practices, regulations, and operations of a program; and (3) provide experience in using the specific procedures of automated accounting systems to find, review, or change accounting data in automated files of transactions, ledgers, accounts, summary reports and financial statements.

OR

D. Completion of a combination of education and experience as described in A and C above. (Refer to the instructions below on how to combine education and experience.)

GENERAL INFORMATION FOR THE APPLICANT:

Applicants must be a United States citizen

As a condition of employment male applicants born after December 31. 1959, must certify that they have registered with the Selective Service System, or are exempt from having to do so under Selective Service law.

Basis of Rating: No written test is required. Your rating is based on an evaluation of your experience, education, and training, and your responses to the Supplemental Qualifications Statement. Passing score ranges from 70 to 100 before the addition of veterans preference points.

Graduate Education: An academic year of graduate education is considered to be the number of credit hours that your graduate school has determined to represent one academic year of full-time study. Such study may have been performed on a full time or part-time basis. If you cannot obtain your graduate school's definition of one year of graduate study, 18 semester hours (or 27 quarter hours) should be considered as satisfying the requirement for one year of full time graduate study.

Combination of Education and Experience: To combine your education and experience, you must convert each to a percentage and then add the percentages. The combined total of your percentage of education and experience must equal at least 100% in order to qualify. If your education is currently described in quarter hours, convert the quarter hours into semester hours by multiplying the quarter hours by the fraction 2/3. For GS-07: To calculate percentage of graduate education, divide number of graduate semester hours by 18.

Check above for a description of qualifying experience that can be used in this calculation. To determine your percentage of qualifying experience, you must divide your total number of months of qualifying experience by the required number of months of experience. For example, GS-07 requires 12 months of specialized experience as described in "C" above. Now add your percentages of education and experience. The two percentages must total at least 100%.

Postage-paid Envelopes: It is against the law to use Government franked envelopes or mail services to submit application in accordance with 18 USC 1719. Applicants who use official postage-paid envelopes will not receive consideration.

Veterans Preference:A 5 point preference is granted to veterans who entered the military service prior to October 14, 1976, or who have served in a military action for which they received a Campaign Badge or Expeditionary Medal. However, you may be entitled to 10 point veterans preference if you are a disabled veteran; you have received a Purple Heart; your are the spouse or mother of a deceased veterans. If you are claiming 10-point veterans preference, you will need to submit an SF15, Application for 10 Point Veterans' Preference, plus the proof required by that form.

Equal Employment Opportunity: Applications are assured of equal consideration regardless of race, sex, age, religion, color, national origin, lawful political affiliation, marital status, membership or nonmembership in an employee organization, or nondisqualifying physical or mental handicap.

OTHER INFORMATION:

1.   Applicant may be required to travel 25% or more of the time.

2.   Applicant is also subject to the rotational policies of the Naval Audit Service.

3. Position requires a Secret Clearance.

4. Position may require the submission of a Financial Disclosure Statement (SP 450.)

HOW TO APPLY:

Applicants may contact the Employment Information Center on (202) 606-2700, Message Code 901 to obtain application packages for this announcement (See the instruction for obtaining an application package on the first page of this announcement under, CONTACT PHONE NUMBER).

You must submit a resume, an OF 612, Optional Application for Federal Employment, or any other written format you choose (Refer to OF 510, Applying for a Federal Job, for information needed to evaluate your qualifications.); and a college Transcript.

OPM Form 1203-AW, Qualifications & Availability Form (Form C); (DO NOT FOLD OR STAPLE.) We will verify the answers you provide to the questions on the Supplemental Qualifications Statement against the information you provide in other application materials. Any exaggeration of your experience or any attempts to conceal information can result in your removal from a federal job and bar you from seeking future federal employment.

Your DD-214, Certificate of Release or Discharge from Active Duty, and a letter from the Veterans Administration documenting proof of your disability dated within the last 12 months (for applicable veterans).

TO: Office of Personnel Management
       Office of Washington Examining Services
       Attn: Vacancy Announcement Number: WA-BE-5-0581DM
       P.O. Box 14080
       Washington, DC 20044

For hand carried packages, courier, or overnight delivery service, send application package to:

Office of Personnel Management
Office of Washington Examining Services
Attn: Vacancy Announcement Number: WA-BE-5-0581DM
1900 E Street, NW, Room 2469
Washington, DC 20415-0001

COMPLETE APPLICATION PACKAGES MUST BE POSTMARKED ON OR BEFORE THE CLOSING DATE OF THIS ANNOUNCEMENT. Incomplete applications and other related forms may result in your missing consideration for this vacancy. The application and related documents will become the property of the Office of Personnel Management. APPLICATION PACKAGES POSTMARKED AFTER THE CLOSING DATE WILL RESULT IN NONCONSIDERATION FOR THIS POSITION.

RELOCATION EXPENSES WILL NOT BE PAID.

We appreciate your interest in federal employment.

Appendix F
Veterans' Programs

Veterans' Preference for Federal Jobs

By law, veterans who are disabled or who served on active duty in the United States Armed Forces during certain specified time periods or in military campaigns are entitled to preference over nonveterans both in hiring into the federal civil service and in retention during reductions in force. Preference does not apply when a job is filled from within the service by promotion, transfer, or other appropriate means.

Hiring Preference in Civil Service Examinations

The "civil service examination" is the process by which an applicant's qualifications are measured against established standards for a category of jobs or the requirements of a specific job. The examination *may* be a written test resulting in a test score. In such case it is called an "assembled examination," meaning that applicants assemble at set times and places. Assembled examinations are becoming rare for most occupations today. For most jobs, the "examination" is the evaluation of the Optional Application Form 612, the resume, the SF-171, or whatever the applicant chooses to submit as an application. Subject matter experts or personnel officials examine the application. They rate applications for experience, education, training, skills, awards, and other factors.

Candidates who pass an examination are ranked by their scores. Veterans eligible for preference are entitled to have 5 or 10 extra points (explained below) included in their scores if they pass an examination. A passing score is 70 or higher. Regardless of their scores, qualified veterans with a compensable service-connected disability of 10 percent or more are placed at the top of most civil service examination lists of eligibles, except for scientific and professional jobs at GS-9 or higher.

A federal agency hiring candidates from an examination list must consider the top three available candidates for each vacancy. An agency may not pass over a candidate with preference and select an individual without preference who has the same or lower score, unless the Office of Personnel Management approves the agency's reasons.

Veterans may apply within 120 days before or after separation for any examination open during their military service.

5-Point Hiring Preference

Five points are added to the passing examination score of a veteran who served:

- During the period December 7, 1941, to July 1, 1955; or

- For more than 180 consecutive days any part of which occurred after January 31, 1955, and before October 15, 1976; or

- In a campaign or expedition for which a campaign medal has been authorized, including Lebanon, Grenada, Panama, and Southwest Asia (Desert Shield/Storm).

Medal holders who enlisted after September 7, 1980, or entered on active duty on or after October 14, 1982, must have served continuously for 24 months or the full period called or ordered to active duty. This service requirement does not apply to veterans with compensable service-connected disabilities, or to veterans separated for disability in the line of duty, or for hardship.

10-Point Hiring Preference

Ten points are added to the passing examination score of:

- A veteran who served at any time and who (1) has a present service-connected disability or (2) is receiving compensation, disability, retirement benefits, or pension from the military or the Department of Veterans Affairs. Individuals who received a Purple Heart qualify as disabled veterans.

- An unmarried spouse of certain deceased veterans, a spouse of a veteran unable to work because of a service-connected disability, and a mother of a veteran who dies in service or who is permanently and totally disabled.

Ten-point preference eligibles may apply for any job for which (1) a list of examination eligibles is (or is about to be) established, or (2) a non-temporary appointment was made in the last 3 years.

General Requirements for Preference

Preference applies in hiring from civil service examinations, for most excepted service jobs, and when agencies make temporary appointments, or use direct hire and delegated examining authorities from OPM. Here are the general requirements:

- An honorable or general discharge is necessary.

- Military retirees at the rank of major, lieutenant commander, or higher are not eligible for preference, except disabled veterans.

- Guard or Reserve active duty for training purposes does *not* qualify for preference.

When applying for federal jobs, eligible veterans claim preference on their job applications. (Applicants claiming 10-point preference must complete form SF 15, Application for 10-Point Veteran Preference.)

Thirty Percent or More Disabled Veterans

Veterans with 30 percent or higher compensable service-connected disability ratings are eligible for direct appointments without examination, which may lead to conversions to career appointments. Veterans should contact the federal agencies where they would like to work for job opportunity information.

If rejected for employment or retention because of disability or if passed over for hiring, these veterans are entitled to be notified by the agency, to respond to the agency's action, and to receive a copy of OPM's final determination. Once hired, disabled veterans can participate in the Disabled Veterans Affirmative Action Program and receive assistance in development and advancement opportunities.

Credit for Military Service

When a candidate's work experience is evaluated in an examination, full credit is given for military service. Such service is either considered as an extension of the work the veteran did before entering the Armed Forces, or it is rated on the basis of the actual duties performed in the Armed

Forces, whichever is more beneficial to the veteran. Also military time any count toward civil service retirement and vacations.

Retention Preference

Generally, employees who have preference in examinations and appointments also have preference over other employees in retaining their jobs in a reduction in force (RIF). However, certain employees who retired from military service are not eligible for preference for job retention purposes.

When layoffs are necessary, each nontemporary employee competes for retention with other employees who do similar work at the same pay grade and who serve under similar conditions. Among competing employees, the order of separation is determined by type of appointment, veterans preference, length of service, and performance ratings.

Veterans have preference in retention over nonveterans. Veterans with disability ratings of 30 percent or higher or whose performance has been rated acceptable have preference over nonveterans and other veterans.

Veterans Readjustment Appointments

By law, federal agencies may hire qualified veterans of the Armed Forces directly under the Veterans Readjustment Appointment (VRA) program. VRA appointees initially are hired for a 2-year period in the excepted service. Successful completion of the VRA leads to a permanent civil service appointment in the competitive service.

Are You Eligible?

You are eligible for a VRA if you served for a period of more than 180 days active duty, all or part of which occurred after August 4, 1964, and have other than a dishonorable discharge.

How Long Are You Eligible?

If you served on active duty between August 5, 1964, and May 7, 1975, you have either 10 years after the date of your last separation from active duty, or until December 31, 1995, whichever is later. If you have a service-connected disability of 30 percent or more, you have no time limit.

What Kind of Jobs Are Available?

Agencies can use the VRA authority to fill jobs up through GS-11 and equivalent jobs under other pay systems. The agency you apply to decides whether you meet the experience and education requirements for the job it wants to fill. Agencies may require passing a test for some jobs.

How Do You Apply?

Contact the personnel office at the federal agency where you want to work to find out what jobs are available. Agencies can recruit candidates and make VRAs directly without using OPM examination lists. If you need career development help, contact your local State Employment Service or Department of Veterans Affairs office.

Is the VRA Program Mandatory for Agencies?

No, it is an optional program. VRA eligibles are not guaranteed appointment. When agencies have vacancies to fill, they can choose candidates from civil service examination lists, agency employees, or current and former federal employees with civil service status. The VRA program gives agencies another source to consider for selecting quality candidates. An agency picks the candidate it believes can do the job best.

Do Disabled Veterans Get Special Consideration?

Yes. When hiring under the VRA program, agencies must give preference consideration to disabled veterans and others with veterans' preference over veterans who are not eligible for preference.

Will You Receive Training?

If you have less than 15 years of formal education, agencies are required to provide a training program for you. If you have 15 years or more, you may participate in training programs on the same basis as other employees. A training program could include on-the-job assignments or classroom training.

What If You Did Not Serve Long Enough?

The requirement for more than 180 days active service does not apply to (1) veterans separated from active duty because of a service-connected disability, or (2) reserve and guard members who served on active duty during a period of war, such as the Persian Gulf War, or in a military operation for which a campaign or expeditionary medal is authorized.

For More Information

Veterans may call or visit Federal Employment Information Centers. Check your local phone directory under U.S. Government. Ask for the specialist who answers inquiries from veterans.

WORK EXPERIENCE

Describe your paid nonpaid work experience related to the job for which you are applying. Do not attach job descriptions.

Job title (if Federal, include series and grade)

From (MM/YY)	To (MM/YY)	Salary $	per	Hours per week

Employer's name and address | Supervisor's name and phone ( )

Describe your duties and accomplishments

WORK EXPERIENCE

Describe your paid nonpaid work experience related to the job for which you are applying. Do not attach job descriptions.

Job title (if Federal, include series and grade)

From (MM/YY)	To (MM/YY)	Salary $	per	Hours per week

Employer's name and address | Supervisor's name and phone ( )

Describe your duties and accomplishments

WORK EXPERIENCE

Describe your paid nonpaid work experience related to the job for which you are applying. Do not attach job descriptions.

Job title (if Federal, include series and grade)	
From (MM/YY) To (MM/YY) Salary per $	Hours per week
Employer's name and address	Supervisor's name and phone ( )

Describe your duties and accomplishments

Index

The Book of U.S. Government Jobs: *Where They Are, What's Available, and How to Get One,* 6th Ed., by Dennis Damp
$18.95, 1995, 256 pages

The federal hiring system changed significantly in 1994. Entire programs were eliminated or streamlined. Damp, an advisor for America On-Line's Federal Career Center, provides a detailed view of the new federal employment system which has more employees that the top 16 Fortune 500 companies combined. The all new 6th edition is an easy to follow, step-by-step guide to high-paying jobs with the U.S. government. Filled with everything you need to know about obtaining a federal government job, this book guides you through Uncle Sam's unique hiring world.

"An updated, comprehensive how-to-guide. Written in a clear, readable style, this book is Recommended."

— LIBRARY JOURNAL

Applying for Federal Jobs: *A Guide to Writing Successful Applications and Resumes for the Job You Want in Government,* by Patricia B. Wood

$17.95, 1995, 224 page

Starting in 1995, job hunters may now use resumes or new simplified optional forms to apply for federal jobs. Learn how to write a professional federal resume and application, use government buzz words, and develop job search strategies that work to land the job you want in government. You'll learn how to develop viable job search strategies and to write applications and resumes that shout:

★ Hire me. I'm the best person for the job! ★

"What a timely book—just what is needed to successfully apply for a federal job or write an effective resume. This is a valuable resource for first-time job seekers and federal employees seeking promotions, lateral transfers, or detail assignments. I highly recommend it!"

—**Frank T. Davis**, President, Frank T. Davis Associates, and former Special Assistant to the Comptroller General of the United States

Health Care Job Explosion! *Career In The 90's* by Dennis V. Damp.
$14.95, 1993, 384 pages

The health care job market is **EXPLODING**. Currently, seven out of every one hundred Americans work in health services. By the year 2005 that figure will increase to nine out of every one hundred, that's **3,900,000 NEW JOBS!**

Health Care Job Explosion! by Dennis V. Damp is a comprehensive **career guide** and **job finder** that steers readers to where they can actually find job openings; periodicals with job ads, placement services, directories, associations, job fairs, and job hotlines. All major health care groups are explored including the nature of work for each occupation, describing:

- Typical working conditions
- Training/advancement potential
- Job outlook and earnings

- Employment opportunities
- Necessary qualifications
- Related occupations

PLUS more than 1,000 verified job resources

"...this book will be a boon to those seeking jobs. Well rounded... Recommended for general collections; this book will be in demand.   — **LIBRARY JOURNAL**

Air Conditioning & Refrigeration Technician's EPA Certification Guide: Getting Certified, Understanding the Rules, & Preparing for EPA Inspections by James Preston
$29.95, 1994, 192 pages

Learn from an expert. The author, James Preston — certified universal technician — passed the **Type I, II, III, and Universal** exams on his first try using the techniques presented in this book. All air conditioning and refrigeration technicians now require certification by the EPA.

This certification and inspection primer teaches service technicians, those planning to enter the field, and business owners about the 1990 Clean Air Act's refrigerant recycling rules and prepares them for the certification test and on-site EPA inspections. This guide prepares technicians, students, and businesses for Clean Air Act implementation and includes:

- Certification Test Preparation
- Training Plan Development
- Freon Recovery/Recycling
- Labeling Requirements
- Complete References

- EPA InspectionGuidance
- Closed Book Practice Exams
- EPA Record Keeping Requirements
- Hundreds of Sample Test Questions
- The History Behind Ozone Depletion

*"...Since the announcement of EPA regs mandating technician testing last fall, there has been a tremendous demand for a guidebook which will 'do it all': get your employees certified, get your equipment in order, and make sure you're OK with the EPA... **This book may be your best resource you have, short of a paid consultant. A valuable book.**"*

— **REFRIGERATION News**